THE GUINNESS BOOK OF

HUMOROUS GAFFES

Colin Jarman

GUINNESS PUBLISHING

This publication © Guinness Publishing Limited (1996),
33 London Road, Enfield, Middlesex

Reprint 10 9 8 7 6 5 4 3 2 1 0

Text design and layout: Amanda Ward

Cover design: DH Publicity

Printed and bound in Great Britain by Cox & Wyman Ltd, Reading

A catalogue record for this book is available from the British Library.

ISBN 0-85112-548-4

CONTENTS

An A-Z of Gaffes 5

Foreign translations 147

What did they mean? 154

Index 156

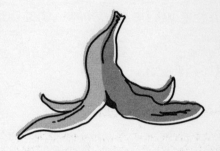

I stand by all the misstatements.
Vice President Dan Quayle

I say some things, and gosh, I wish I hadn't said them.
Hubert H. Humphrey

Our first move will be to decide what our first move will be.
Wellington Mara

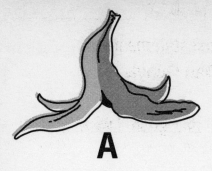

A

ACTING UP

Gene Tierney - she's a woman actress.
James McGauley
(1994)

Actor sent to jail for not finishing sentence.
***El Paso Times* headline**

All we want, like Marlene Dietrich, is to be alone.
Jack Rowell
(1995)

Baseball without fans is like Jayne Mansfield without a sweater.
President Richard Nixon

Serge Blanco is on the floor, trying to win an A.B.T.A. award for acting.
Steve Smith, ITV World Cup rugby
(1991)

ADVICE

Pitch it up more. You've got to catch the batsman in two man's land.
Ken Barrington

To clean your oven put ammonia and water in a pan and sit in the oven.
Daytona Daily News

Experienced fencers occasionally spend a few minutes giving pointers to beginners.
Albert Manley, *Complete Fencing*
(1979)

Let's have spontaneous fun, and here's how.
Singapore Times

If you can't stand the heat in the dressing room, get out of the kitchen.
Terry Venables, Capital Gold
(1995)

AGE-OLD QUESTION

Half the population is aged over 40, not under.
Lauren Bacall

I was 18 about six years ago - I'm 28 now.
Frank Bruno

Moses Kiptanui - the 19-year-old Kenyan, who turned 20 a few weeks ago.
David Coleman, BBC TV athletics

He's 31 this year, last year he was 30.
David Coleman, BBC TV sport

Kevin Reeves, who's just turned 22, proving that an ill wind blows nobody no good.
David Coleman, BBC TV football

He certainly looks older than he did last year.
Mark Cox, BBC TV tennis

He must have discovered euthanasia. He never seems to get any older.
John Francome, Channel 4 Racing

Bruce Sutter has been around a while, and he's pretty old. He's 35 years old. That will give you an idea of how old he is.
Ron Fairly, US TV baseball

The average age of the White Sox team is 26 years per man.
Ken Brett, US TV baseball

Well Kerry, you're 19 and you're a lot older than a lot of people younger than yourself.
Mike Gray

My seven year old who is now ten.
Lady Olga Maitland MP

ALL THE PRESIDENT'S MEND

Ronald Reagan has lost his head over President Carter ... Ronald Reagan has lost his LEAD over President Carter.
**Anon. newsreader, BBC Radio World Service
(1980)**

President Ronald Reagan is alive and well and kicking tonight, one day after the assassination attempt, just two months into his pregnancy.
Anon. US TV newscaster

There were many highs and lows during the Reagan's eight years at the White House ... low points like cancer. And perhaps the lowest of them all, when President Reagan survived an assassination attempt.
John Dunn, BBC Radio 2

As the Reagan presidency ends, it is time for the Bush pregnancy to begin.
Governor Tommy Thompson of Wisconsin

Mr Bush is the first living US President to visit Czechoslovakia.
Voice of America

The first black President will be a politician who is black.
Governor L. Douglas Wilder of Virginia

I believe, that next to God, Andrew Jackson was the greatest man who ever lived.
John T. Moore

I have my own opinions, strong opinions, but I don't always agree with them.
President George Bush

ALONE AGAIN

A bachelor's life is not for a single man.
Samuel Goldwyn

The single, overwhelming two facts are ...
Paddy Ashdown MP

Single misfortunes never come alone, and the greatest of all national calamities is generally followed by one greater.
Sir Boyle Roche MP

ANON US LECTURERS

You mustn't be too rigid when doing fluid mathematics.

It's dangerous to name your children until you know how many you are going to have.

Who should be doing this computer course? Everyone apart from the third year of the two-year CompSci course.

You don't have to copy that down, there's no wisdom in it. It only repeats what I said.

I need to use an immediately distinguishable character ... so I'll use something that no one will recognize.

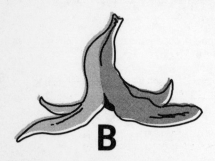

B

BAD TIMING

Bandleaders come and go, but the perennial Duke Ellington, like Tennyson's brook, seems destined to go on forever.
Bath and West Evening Chronicle
(1974)
(The Duke died the following day)

Dizzy Gillespie is the most genial elder statesman of jazz ... and a great survivor.
Ian Carr, BBC Music
(February 1993)
(Dizzy died in January 1993)

Pantani has been called the Kojak of cycling. I wonder if Telly Savalas is watching on E.S.P.N. back in America?
David Duffield, Tour de France, Channel 4
(1995)
(Telly Savalas died in 1994)

BAIRD BRAINED

In this country we take a paternalistic view of television, hence the great name 'Auntie Beeb'.
Michael Grade

On Friday, when he retired, Mr Reber was presented with a portable television and a pair of binoculars.
Essex Country Standard

BEAST BEHAVIOUR

Yorkshire man takes Supreme Pig title.
***Harrogate Advertiser* headline**

Woman is Sheep Dog champion.
***The Guardian* headline**
(1977)

Outed RSPCA Man Says He Was A Scapegoat.
***The Times* headline**

Everything for your pets. Send a s.a.e. for ill. cat.
Anon. Shropshire newspaper advert (for a pet shop)

I ain't no great showman. I ain't going to get flash and talk the ass of a donkey.
Frank Bruno
(1986)

A squid as you know has ten testicles.
Graham Kerr, *The Galloping Gourmet*

We've already hunted the grey whale into extinction twice.
Andrea Arnold
(1990)

Dead Cats Protest.
***Daily Telegraph* headline**

Journalists sometime write what I say and not what I mean.
Pedro Guerrero

In the next programme, we'll be looking at blind dogs for the guide.
Simon Groom, *Blue Peter*, BBC TV

My house was swept away clean and so was my barn. I had some mules in the barn but they tell me they didn't get hurt.
Memphis Commercial Appeal

Ian Rush headed the third goal near the end, having hit the bear earlier.
The Guardian

Jack Russell was LBW, bowled Geoff Lawson for a typically dogged 42.
Dominic Allen

Sporting Lisbon in their green and white hoops, looking like a team of zebras.
Peter Jones, BBC Radio football

Just enough points on the table for Tony Knowles to pull the cat out of the fire.
Ray Edmonds, BBC TV snooker

BIBLICAL PROPORTIONS

The beauty of cup football is that Jack always has a chance of beating Goliath.
Terry Cooper
(1993)

Halifax and Spurs - the original David against Goliath.
John Helm, ITV football

Simpson slew the Philippines.
President Ronald Reagan

He took the Cup and He broke it.
Anon. Aberystwyth cleric

Our Father who art in Havant.
Anon. Portsmouth schoolboy

If English was good enough for Jesus Christ, it's good enough for me.
Anon. US Congressman

God Bless The Holy Trinity.
Anon. Irish banner

BIRD'S NEST SCOOP

British Bird Men Held By Turkey.
Daily Telegraph headline

It rolls off my back like a duck.
Samuel Goldwyn

Biggin Hill police investigating the theft have asked pet shops in the area to be on the lookout for canaries going cheap.
Kentish Times

Deputy Sweetman had better give up pretending to be a cuckoo sitting on a mare's nest.
Sean MacEntee, Irish politician

Jurgen Klinsmann has taken to English football like a duck out of water.
**Gerry Francis, Grandstand, BBC TV
(1995)**

An ostrich that turns a blind eye to the other aspects of the hobby will inevitably become a boomerang.
Handyman

Everyone in the town hall is wandering around like headless chickens looking over their shoulders to see if they are going to be next.
Anon. Hackney local government officer

Hero Raaj Kumar has been asking for it and he is getting it in the neck. At last, the chickens have come home to roast for him.
Bangladesh Times

The Government has really put the clay among the pigeons.
Brian Redhead, BBC Radio 4

This could well be the goose that killed the golden egg.
Anon. Chester city councillor

A man could not be in two places at the same time unless he were a bird.
Sir Boyle Roche MP

BLAME EXCUSE

We've only one person to blame and that's each other.
Barry Beck

I don't blame anyone, except perhaps all of us.
William Whitelaw MP

BODY OF EVIDENCE

On being hit by Bob Fitzsimmons:
Solar plexus be damned! It was a belly punch!
James J. Corbett

There must be something on Gooch's mind, and he wants to get it off his chest.
Farokh Engineer, BBC TV cricket

That's no hair of my chest.
Martina Navratilova

Miss World is still popular even though it has its fair share of knockers.
Julia Morley, co-organizer of the Miss World competition

Young lady required in accounts office, previous experience not essential busts must be able to type.
Portsmouth Evening Echo

Ann's Two Boobs Sink Britain.
Daily Mirror headline
(1970)

We have often in the past had Wimbledon wobbles with nervy players so shaky that their boobs have sometimes made park players blush.
Daily Express

Steve Cram may appear cool and relaxed but inside there burns a heart of steel.
Dave Moorcroft, BBC Radio 4
(1988)

Upon being asked about the racial question:
Sure, I look like a white man but my heart is as black as anybody's heart.
Governor George Wallace of Alabama
(1971)

Henry Rono, the man with asbestos lungs.
Ron Pickering, BBC TV athletics

After banging your head against a brick wall for long enough you'd think that some of it would rub off.
Alex Murphy, BBC TV rugby league

He looks up at him through his blood-smeared lips.
Harry Carpenter, BBC TV boxing

The only luxury is freedom, freedom of the mind. They can chop off my head and take everything else as long as they leave me that.
Dieter Meier

The forwards shot hard and often but never straight, till at last Hill decided to try his head. It came off first time.
Anon. Kent newspaper

I think I can scotch that one on the head right away.
Sir Jeremy Thomas

Brain damage is always on a boxer's mind.
Anon. Irish boxer

He's got a little notch in his brain which he turns off.
Frank Bruno

I should like to retire from boxing with my brains intact.
Herol Graham

He's one of those footballers whose brains are in his head.
**Derek Johnstone, BBC TV Scotland
(1994)**

Graeme Souness's brain working at 100 mph out there.
Brian Moore, ITV football

Artificial Limbs Centre Has New Head.
***Indian Express* headline**

He held his head in his hands as it flashed past the post.
**Alan Brazil, BBC Radio 5
(1995)**

I'm putting my head up, but if it's shot off, it's no skin off my back.
**David Arblaster
(1978)**

Steve Robinson, the former champion, has seen his crown slip from his shoulders.
**Paul Dempsey, Sky Sports boxing
(1995)**

He can talk over the heads of the intelligentsia to grass roots level.
John Brown

Greg Page controlled the temple of the fight.
Renaldo Snipes

Aberdeen are taking this bitter pill on the chin.
Anon. football commentator

The Romanians certainly aren't going to lie down and take it on the chin.
**Rupert Moon, Eurosport World Cup rugby
(1995)**

I felt a lump in my throat as the ball went in.
Terry Venables, ITV football

They pushed their nomination down my throat behind my back.
J. Ramsay MacDonald, Prime Minister

Stuart Pearce has got the taste of Wembley in his nostrils.
John Motson, BBC TV football
(1991)

Don't cut off your nose yourself.
Charles 'Casey' Stengel

Eye witnesses were on the scene in minutes.
Adam Boulton

Edwards missed getting Stearns at third base by an eyeball.
Jerry Coleman, US TV baseball

Everything that this Government has done must be wrong in Deputy Brasier's eyes. He views everything through red, white and blue glasses.
Martin Corry

If I took off my sunglasses, everyone could see that I was lying through my teeth.
George Michael

It is no use for the honourable Member to shake his head in the teeth of his own words.
William E. Gladstone, Prime Minister

The identity of a headless corpse found in a woodland near Liskeard will not be positively known until dental records have been checked.
Western Morning News

I wish the critics would stop knocking David Gower. It really annoys me the way he is kicked in the teeth every time his back is turned.
A. Daniels, Letter to Daily Star

It's at times like this that you have to clench your teeth together and say a prayer.
Ted Lowe, BBC TV snooker

St Helens have really got their tail between their teeth.
Malcolm Lord

They were laughing at everybody behind their faces.
Simon Bates

The pale face of the British soldier is the backbone of our Indian army.
Anon. Scottish MP

These people haven't seen the last of my face. If I go down, I'm going down standing up.
Chuck Person

There's a very sad Wattana, but you'd never know it to look at his face.
Ted Lowe, BBC TV snooker

We are sitting on a powderkeg that could explode in our faces at any time.
Archbishop Desmond Tutu

Perhaps the murderous martial law men would break in, cut us into joints, and throw our bleeding heads on the tables to stare us in the face.
Sir Boyle Roche MP

£8000 Facelift For Westerham Sportswomen.
Sevenoaks News
(1979)

What a picture! It will be a feather in your eye.
Harry Rapf

On the mound is Randy Jones, the left-hander with the Karl Mark hair-do.
Jerry Coleman, US TV baseball

When I see the pictures you [Louis B. Mayer] play in the theatre, it makes the hair stand on the edge of my seat.
Michael Curtiz

Obviously for Scunthorpe, it would be a nice scalp to put Wimbledon on our bottoms.
Dave Bassett
(1987)

It is possible to travel to New York or London on Concorde with the other leg on the QE2.
The Times

A competition is to take place to determine the owners of the best three pairs of legs in Vienna.
Evening News

Fred Davis, the doyen of snooker, now 67 years of age and too old to get his leg over, prefers to use his left hand.
Ted Lowe, BBC TV snooker

Celtic manager David Hay still has a fresh pair of legs up his sleeve.
John Greig
(1986)

Smith Breaks Leg In Third Leg.
***Guardian* headline in sailing section**

My legs sort of disappeared from nowhere.
Chris Waddle

From the waist down, Earl Campbell has the biggest legs I've ever seen on a running back.
John Madden, CBS TV US football

It's just like a knee injury - except it's in the head.
Ray Perkins

Use of the elbow has crept into football over the last few years and should be stamped out.
**George Best, Sky TV football
(1993)**

Once Tony Daley opens his legs, you've got a problem.
Howard Wilkinson

Willie Carson, riding his 180th winner of the season, spent the last two furlongs looking over one shoulder then another, even between his legs, but there was nothing there to worry him.
Sporting Life

This summer, in the long jump, I'll let my legs do the talking.
**Stuart Faulkner
(1988)**

Once again, we got a good kick up the backside. Maybe it's the shot in the arm we needed.
**Allan Border
(1992)**

I wouldn't say that Joe Namath has a sore arm ... but his arm is kind of sore.
Weeb Ewbank

Being naturally right-footed he doesn't often chance his arm with his left foot.
Trevor Brooking, BBC TV football

Geoff Hurst had a hammer in his left boot and good left feet are like bricks of gold.
Jimmy Greaves

We want to produce dancers who at 16 can walk into the Royal Ballet School and stand on their own two feet.
Daily Telegraph

England batsmen will never get many runs if they persist in sitting on their back foot.
**Sir Len Hutton
(1979)**

Businessmen should stand or fall on their own two feet.
Edwina Currie MP

On Charlton Athletic's promotion prospects:
We're halfway round the Grand National course with many hurdles to clear. So let's make sure we keep our feet firmly on the ground.
Mike Bailey
(1981)
(The Grand National is a steeplechase and has fences not hurdles.)

If you find you're in hot water, put your best foot forward.
Ann O'Neill

Right now, I feel that I've got my feet on the ground as far as my head is concerned.
Bo Belinsky

The ball was glued to his foot - all the way into the back of the net.
Alan Parry, ITV football
(1990)

If you kick the feet from under an infant you may put it on a sound basis.
Patrick McGilligan

The Deputy has the habit of shutting his mouth after putting his foot in it.
Sean F. Lemass TD

Not only is he ambidextrous, but he can throw with either hand.
Duffy Daugherty

Mickey Mantle can hit just as good right-handed as he can left- handed. He's just naturally amphibious.
Lawrence 'Yogi' Berra

Mike Caldwell, the Padres' right-handed southpaw, will pitch for San Diego tonight.
Jerry Coleman, US TV baseball

Yes, my wife's hands are very beautiful. I'm going to have a bust made of them.
Samuel Goldwyn

Pat Jennings' hands are so large, from his thumb to his fingertips was a foot.
Steve Ryder, BBC TV football

Otto Preminger had his wrist on the pulse of the world.
Vincent Price

Monica Seles has so much control of the racket with those double-handed wrists.
Virginia Wade, BBC TV tennis

BOTTOMS UP

Multi-millionaire sex king Paul Raymond wants to buy Watford, the English
First Division's bottom club.
Gulf Daily News

By common consent these were males prostituting themselves for
money - people at the bottom end of their trade.
The Times

Let's nip this thing in the butt.
Bill Peterson

Do you scratch your bottom while taking a bath? Have it reglazed by the
professionals.
Edinburgh Advertiser

BOX OF TRICKS

I suppose if you let this genie out of the bottle, you'd get a whole lot of
butterflies out of Pandora's box.
Pru Goward

It's a can of worms full of Pandora's box.
Alan Watkins

As we debate this Bill, that sword of Damocles is hanging over Pandora's
box.
Anon. New York City councillor

If you open that Pandora's box you never know what Trojan 'orses will
jump out.
Ernest Bevin MP

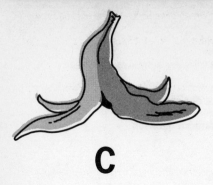

C

CAPITAL PUNISHMENT

I'm for a stronger death penalty.
President George Bush

I favour capital punishment. It saves lives.
Nancy Reagan

Life is indeed precious, and I believe the death penalty helps to affirm this fact.
Mayor Ed Koch of New York

Death by hanging was the penalty for murder in mainland Britain until 1965, when it was temporarily suspended. Suspension was made permanent in 1970.
The Guardian

Now, we are continuing our extended phone-in on the death penalty, and I already have the Reverend Ian Paisley hanging on the line.
Brian Redhead, BBC Radio 4

Capital punishment is our society's recognition of the sanctity of human life.
Senator Orrin Hatch of Utah

CASE FOR THE DEFENCE

We are not at war with Egypt. We are in an armed conflict.
Sir Anthony Eden, Prime Minister
(1956)

Our troops advanced today without losing a foot of ground.
British Army report

We were not microgramming Grenada intelligencewise until about the same time.
US Admiral W.L. MacDonald

The only way we'll ever get a volunteer army is to draft them.
F.E. Hebert

Military order during the Battle of Alabama:
Elevate them guns a little lower.
**General, later President, Andrew Jackson
(1815)**

CHILD'S PLAY

Successful breast-feeding, an evening for everyone.
Advert for St Austell Health Office in *Cornish Guardian*

If you need something to take your mind off breast-feeding, the place to be was Bristol.
Jenni Murray, BBC Radio 4

Three day boat trip to Denmark. Kids we throw in for free.
News of the World

Children who reach school age multiply at an average of 30,000 per day.
Egyptian Gazette

Mothers' help wanted to help with children and lighthouse work.
East Grinstead newspaper

So Carol, you're a housewife and a mother. Have you got any children?
Michael Barrymore

Bringing up children on your own is very difficult, even when there are two parents.
Virginia Bottomley MP

Music, sex and family are my greatest pleasures. Sex and family are the same things to me.
Simon Le Bon

My mum said I used to fight my way out of the cot. But I can't remember. That was before my time.
Frank Bruno

Little children who could neither walk nor talk were running about in the streets cursing their Maker.
Sir Boyle Roche MP

We were able to slow down and dilute child care.
Senator Robert Dole

COCK UP

I am not wanting to make too long speech tonight, as I am knowing your old English saying, 'Early to bed and up with the cock'.
Anon. Hungarian diplomat

Ah! Isn't that nice, the wife of the Cambridge president is kissing the cox of the Oxford crew.
Harry Carpenter, BBC TV boat race
(1977)

Cox are cox no matter what sex they are.
President of the Oxford Boat Race Union
(1981)

Watch out for the free supplement in next month's issue: Brides' First Cockery Course.
Anon. woman's magazine

The judge in the IRA bomb trial is feared to be high on the terrorist's hit list ... and could face months of around-the-cock protection of Special Branch.
Belfast Telegraph

The British boys are adopting the attacking position - Cox up at the net.
Dan Maskell, BBC TV tennis

It was the 73rd career Grand Prick title for McEnroe.
China Daily

Replying to Walter Mondale's charge that "He doesn't have the manhood to apologize" :
Well, on the manhood thing, I'll put mine up against his any time.
President George Bush

COLOUR BLIND

He's going for the pink, and for those of you with black-and-white sets, the yellow is behind the blue.
Ted Lowe, BBC TV snooker

For those of you watching in black-and-white, Spurs are in the all-yellow strip.
John Motson, BBC TV football
(1978)

All the Brazilian supporters are wearing yellow shirts. It's a fabulous kaleidoscope of colour.
John Motson, BBC TV football

It's been every colour under the rainbow.
Toyah Wilcox

Nick Faldo this afternoon in all-blue, with a white shirt.
Tony Adamson

The all-white suits of this German ski team make them look so very colourful.
Emlyn Jones, ITV skiing
(1979)

Gilbert hit a kamikaze back-pass which Fashanu pounced on like a black Frank Bruno.
Ian Darke, Sky TV football

It's Great Britain in the all-white strip with the red and blue V, the dark shorts and the dark stockings.
Ray French, Sky TV rugby

It's a good job I'm not colour-blind, because both teams are playing in black and white.
Harry Gratian, BBC TV rugby

Manchester United are buzzing around the goalmouth like a lot of red bluebottles.
David Coleman, BBC TV football

You'll be able to read it in black and white tomorrow, and if you get the Financial Times, you'll see it in pink and white.
Dominic Harrod

Wembley Way is beginning to blacken with people in terms of red and blue.
Alan Jackson

Paul Azinger is wearing an all-black outfit: black jumper, blue trousers, white shoes and a pink teacosy hat.
Renton Laidlaw

CONTRA DICTION

The slalom champion Ingmar Stenmark does not ski Downhill.
Frank Bough, BBC TV skiing

All I was doing was appealing for an endorsement, not suggesting you endorse it.
President George Bush

The whole defence stopped as one man, Armitage in particular.
Brian Moore, ITV football

These are the sort of doors that get opened if you don't close them.
Terry Venables

They've given it all tonight, but there's a little left to give.
Harry Carpenter, BBC TV boxing

I'll give you a definite maybe.
Samuel Goldwyn

Don't fail to miss tomorrow's game.
Jay 'Dizzy' Dean,US TV baseball

You have reached the turning point on a voyage of no return.
Simon Bates

The French selectors never do anything by halves; for the first international of the season against Ireland they had dropped half the three-quarter line.
Nigel Starmer-Smith, BBC TV rugby
(1974)

I don't like to look back in retrospect.
Vince Ferragamo

You just can't let nature run wild.
Governor Walter Hickel of Alaska

I'm not saying they're a great team, but they're excellent.
Ron Atkinson, ITV football
(1994)

DAVID COLEMAN

In the UK, mention the word gaffe and most people automatically think of one man, David Coleman. The BBC TV sports commentator has become a legend in his own lead-time - like Goldwyn, Spooner and the fictional Mrs Malaprop, he has even lent his name to a form of gaffe ... Colemanballs.

Private Eye magazine, who christened the new form of gaffe, was also concerned with other aspects of Coleman's delivery, *"I am organizing an expedition to discover the whereabouts of David Coleman. For some time now the BBC have only been using repeats of his voice. No one can deny David is unique and that our children are now being corrupted by the occasional use of five-letter words. If educationalists are to gain influence over BBC Sport and allow the use of good English again we will be forced into (having) a literate Minister of Sport."*

Others viewers have also become worried by the cryptic content of Coleman's commentaries:

"Watching the BBC is something deeper, something occult, something to do with David Coleman's personality. Just by being so madly keen, he helps you get things in proportion. Anything that matters so much to David Coleman, you realize, doesn't matter so much at all."
Clive James *The Observer* (1978)

"What is the most popular sport in Britain today? a. darts b. fishing c. betting d. travelling on the Tube without a ticket e. sports quizzes f. making up remarks supposed to have been said by David Coleman?"
Miles Kington

In defence of David Coleman and all sports commentators, it must be stressed that describing hours of live sporting action is as verbally hazardous as attempting Slovakian tongue-twisters with a mouthful of marbles. The case against mumble-mouthed sports announcers is the simple fact that they are professionals and a gaffe, live or not, must be considered the equal of an own goal or treading on your own wicket. If gaffes were an Olympic sport, David Coleman would be Paavo Nurmi.

Athletics

It's a great advantage to be able to hurdle with both legs.

Lasse Viren, the Olympic champion, came in fifth and ran a champion's race.

In a moment we hope to see the pole vault over the satellite.

This could be a repeat of what will happen at the European Games, next week.

There's a mistake on the scoreboard. They're only showing his Christian names - Ismail Ibrahim.

She's not Ben Johnson, but then who is?

Football

Don't tell those coming in the final result of that fantastic match, but let's have another look at Italy's winning goal.

The ball has broken 50-50 for Kevin Keegan.

General

This is a young man who is only 25, and you have to say, he answered every question that has ever been asked.

In fairness, David Coleman is perhaps best remembered for the one gaffe he didn't utter, at the 1976 Montreal Olympics, "Here comes Juantorena. Watch him open his legs and show his class!". Coleman's co-commentator that day, Ron Pickering, was the guilty party.

They wouldn't have won if we had beaten them.
Lawrence 'Yogi' Berra

When you're not winning, it's tough to win a game.
Tony LaRussa

Journalists sometimes write what I say and not what I mean.
Pedro Guerrero

Our comedies are not to be laughed at.
Samuel Goldwyn

Suddenly, Alex Higgins was 7-0 down.
David Vine, BBC TV snooker

During the Bosnia conflict :
You can't expect the Rapid Reaction Force to be ready immediately.
**Anon. military spokesman, *Today* BBC Radio
(1995)**

Comparing himself to his gaffe-ridden brother Lawrence:
Our similarities are different.
Dale Berra

*Nolan Ryan is pitching much better now he's got his curve ball
straightened out.*
Joe Garagiola, US TV baseball

*There is no such thing as a lack of confidence. You either have it or you
don't.*
Rob Andrew

*It doesn't mean anything, but what it does mean is that Adbe Bile is very
relaxed.*
David Coleman, BBC TV athletics

They came through absolutely together ... with Allan Wells in first place.
David Coleman, BBC TV athletics

There is Brendan Foster, by himself, with 20,000 people.
David Coleman, BBC TV athletics

*Well, Buckhart's in the red. Not only did he play it safely, he played it
dangerously.*
**David Coleman, BBC TV athletics
(1992)**

When Martina Navratlilova is tense it helps her to relax.
Dan Maskell, BBC TV tennis

JERRY COLEMAN

The USA's prime sporting gaffemeister is Jerry Coleman. Jerry is the play-by-play announcer for the San Diego Padres baseball team, who at one time was made team manager, and these are some of his uncut baseball diamonds:

Jesus Alou is in the on-deck circus.

He hits a looping line drive.

Rich Folkers is throwing up in the bullpen.

Davis fouls out to third in fair territory.

All the Padres need is a fly ball in the air.

They throw Winfield out at second, but he's safe.

There's a shot up the alley. Oh, it's just foul.

The first pitch to Tucker Ashford is grounded into left field. No, wait a minute. It's ball one ... low and outside.

Reggie Smith of the Dodgers and Gary Matthews of the homers hit Braves in that game.

If Pete Rose's streak was still intact, with that single to left, the fans would be throwing babies out of the upper deck.

Stay tuned for today's spring training opener against the Angels. This has been the Padres' post-game show.

Gaylord Perry and Willie McCovey should know each other like a book. They've been ex-teammates for years now.

Enos Cabell started out here with the Astros ... and before that he was with the Orioles.

Last night's homer was Willie Stargell's 399th career home run, leaving him one shy of 500.

Those amateur umpires are certainly flexing their fangs tonight.

That noise in my earphone knocked my nose off and I had to pick it up and find it.

At least, David Coleman knows who he is, Jerry once introduced himself thus, *"Hi folks! I'm Gerry Gross".* Gerry Gross is another San Diego baseball announcer!

CONVERSATION PIECES

When you speak to Barry Fry, it's like a thousand piece crossword.
Brian Moore, ITV football
(1996)

It was hard to have a conversation, there were so many people talking.
Lawrence 'Yogi' Berra

CORRECTLY SPEAKING

No responsibility can be accepted for losses arising from typographical errors. Advertisers are expected to check their smalls to ensure correct appearance.
Rhodesia Herald

Our newspaper carried the notice last week that Mr Harmon Jones is a defective in the police force. This was a typographical error - Mr Jones is, of course, a detective in the police farce.
Canaan New Advertiser

Important notice. If you are one of the hundreds of parachuting enthusiasts who bought our Easy Sky Diving booklet, please make the following correction: On page 8, line 7, the words 'state zip code' should have read 'pull rip cord'.
Warrenton Democrat

The Greek Special is a huge 18-inch pizza and not a huge 18-inch penis, as described. Blondie's Pizza would like to apologize for any confusion Friday's ad might have caused.
Daily Californian

An item in Thursday's Nation Digest about the Massachusetts budget crisis made reference to new taxes that will help put Massachusetts 'back in the African American'. The item should have said 'back in the black'.
Fresno Bee

CRIME AND PUNISHMENT

At Oxford Crown Court today, Donald Neilsen denied being the Pink Panther.
Edward Cole, BBC Radio 4

The more killing and homicides you have, the more havoc it prevents.
Mayor Richard J. Daley of Chicago

We are not going to stand idly by and be murdered as we lie in our beds.
Reverend Ian Paisley MP
(1970)

I hope that Spiro Agnew will be completely exonerated and found guilty of the charges against him.
Governor John Connally of Texas
(1973)

Mrs Christine Overy, who was tied to a refrigerator door at gunpoint by two raiders, has been praised for her coolness by Tonbridge police.
Kent Courier

I took one arm, my colleague took the other arm, then we disarmed her.
Anon. policeman, Panorama BBC TV

A set of traffic lights has been stolen from a main road junction in Reading. A police spokesman said, "Some thieves will stop at nothing."
Southend Evening Echo

If the crime in Washington D.C. were down 100 per cent, it would still be 50 times higher than it should be.
John Bowman

CURTIZ-Y CALLS
(the gaffes of film director Michael Curtiz)

This scene has a lot of activity. It is busy like a bee-dive.

To a fragrant actress:
Darling, you stink so beautiful.

To Olivia de Haviland:
Darling, don't fix your hair. It's nice if it's loosey.

Answering his office phone:
I'm out ... but call me back in a hour.

I got a phone call from Jack Warner at one in the morning. He pulled me out of bed. It was a lucky thing I was up playing gin rummy.

This scene will make your blood curl.

To Louis B. Mayer:
When I see the pictures you play in the theatre, it makes the hair stand on the edge of my seat.

Man Shot Dead By Police Station.
Evening Standard headline

If people had proper locks on their doors, crime could be prevented before it happens.
Douglas Hurd MP

The gunmen are reported to have pointed handguns at the heads of the staff in the office and threatened to shoot their kneecaps off.
South London Press

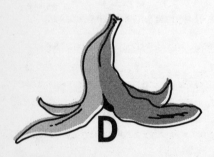

DAIRY

Once the milk has been spilt, in this sort of a case, it's very difficult to put Humpty Dumpty back on the wall again.
Anon. solicitor

A cow may be drained dry, and if the Chancellors of the Exchequer persist in meeting every deficiency that occurs by taxing the brewing and distilling industries, they will inevitably kill the cow that lays the golden milk.
Sir Frederick Milner MP

THE DAY TODAY

Well, the day began this morning.
Tony Greig, Channel 9 TV
(1981)

Ray Wilkins' day will come one night.
Bobby Robson
(1985)

It's a beautiful day for a night game.
Frank Frisch, US TV baseball

And now, as the evening wears on, the shadows cast by the floodlights get longer.
Anon. TV commentator

DEAF EARS

Ladies and gentlemen, if this coercion measure is passed, no man in Ireland will be able to speak upon politics unless he is born deaf and dumb.
Lord Charles Russell MP
(1880)

We should turn a deaf ear to any red herring that may be drawn across our path.
Ann O'Neill

So long as Ireland remains silent on this question England will be deaf to our entreaties.
Anon. 19th century Irish politician

DEATH VOLLEY

Report on the UNICEF benefit football game between The Americas and Rest of the World :
A minute's silence for the deceased Honorary President of FIFA Sir Stanley Rous.
Shot against the post by Maradona (57 mins).
FIFA News

On making enquiries at the hospital this afternoon, we learn that the deceased is as well as can be expected.
Jersey Evening Post

When an Englishman wants to get married, to whom does he go? To the clergy. When he wants to get his child baptized, to whom does he go? To the clergy. When he wants to get buried, to whom does go?
William E. Gladstone, Prime Minister

On being told that Jane Austen was dead:
So she wouldn't be available for book signings?
Anon. US publisher
(1995)

How he doesn't get killed more often, I don't know.
David Parkin
(1981)

Para girl to repeat fatal jump.
***World in Runcorn* headline**

Dead body found at cemetery.
***Calcutta Telegraph* headline**

Suicide is a real threat to health in a modern society.
Virginia Bottomley MP
(1994)

I don't want to beat a dead horse to death.
Lee Trevino

Mr Albert Power, surviving member of Britain's oldest brother- and-sister partnership, will be cremated today with full military honours.
Western Mail

Those who survived the San Francisco earthquake said, "Thank God, I'm still alive". But, of course, those who died, their lives will never be the same again.
Representative Barbara Boxer of California
(1989)

During a visit to Jordan:
Tell me, how dead is the Dead Sea?
President George Bush

After the next election, we have to give the third, and I hope the last, deathblow to Home Rule.
Edward Stanley, Earl of Derby

That's the idea of safety play ... to leave your opponent dead on the baulk cushion.
Clive Everton, BBC TV snooker

French railway president quits after second fatal accident.
***Toronto Globe* headline**

Millions of people who have never died before will be killed.
William Shatner [as Captain Kirk], *Star Trek*

Four people were killed, one seriously, and eight more received slight injuries
Tokyo Times

I wish to thank anyone who so kindly assisted in the death of my husband.
Notice in *Nebraska Smoke-Eater*

Smoking kills. If you're killed, you've lost a very important part of your life.
Brooke Shields

You have to treat death like any other part of life.
Tom Sneva
(1977)

DEATH STYLES OF THE RICH AND FAMOUS

Mozart is celebrating the 200th anniversary of his death.
Derek Jameson, BBC Radio 2

Francis Bacon was probably our greatest living painter ... until he died.
Anon. L.B.C. Radio newsreader

Sadly, the immortal Jackie Milburn died today.
Cliff Morgan

Of course, Jim Morrison is dead now, which is a high price to pay for immortality.
Gloria Estefan

Glenn Miller became a legend in his own lifetime due to his early death.
Nicholas Parsons

Jim Reeves died on 31st July 1964, but his career was not affected by his death.
Ed Stewart

Hirohito's Body Moved.
Anon. Edmonton newspaper headline

DEJA VIEW

Things are more like they are now than they have ever been.
President Gerald Ford

If you didn't see Davis against Hendry in the snooker, last night, then you can see it again now.
Anon. TV announcer

The news from the javelin is that it was won by the winning throw that we saw earlier.
David Coleman, BBC TV athletics

That performance would have won him the Gold medal in the championships four years ago, which he won anyway.
Desmond Lynam, BBC TV Olympics

I'd like to be sort of like Lou Boudreau. He does a great job of recapping the play before it happens.
Johnny Logan

I'm hoping we can fight again, or at least have a rematch.
John Conteh

The first time you face up to a googly, you're going to be in trouble if you've never faced one before.
Trevor Bailey

This change of venue will give the Desert Classic Golf tournament a much better chance of being as good as it always has.
Labron Harris
(1979)

DICEMAN COMETH

Saddam Hussein may still have Scud missiles up his sleeve. That could be his last throw of the dice farther down the road.
Anon. newsreader, Grampian TV
(1991)

This is John Major's last desperate throw of the dice and we will ensure it scores a double blank.
Jack Straw MP
(1993)

DISCHORD

Dennis Harris playing solo trumpet in the Bedford Band was awarded the medal for best trombone player in the section.
Leigh Journal

Beethoven had ten children and practised on a spinster in the attic.
Philadelphia Bulletin

A salvo of six shots was fired as six burglars play The Last Post.
Ilford Recorder

They were singing without accompaniment. You know - acapulco.
Gregory Ratoff

You should hear her sing - she's a female Lena Horne.
Joe Pasternak

I've studied the lyrics note by note.
Gary Barlow
(1993)

I used to play the violin when I was younger, but one day I broke the
strings and I just didn't have the guts to play it again.
Duffy Daugherty

DRUG BUST

On reports that an Old Bailey juror smoked pot during a trial:
There is no substance in this story.
Maureen Evans, Deputy Chief Clerk
(1994)

Cannabis Smuggling By Troops. Investigation By Joint Chiefs.
Morning Star headline

The three appeared on the same charge sheet only because each had
admitted smoking cannabis with one of the others. There were no joint
charges.
Shropshire Star

Tuesday Group Speaker - Mr R. Kirby on 'Drugs and Drug Abuse'. There
will be a Bring-and-Buy stall.
Notice on St Edmunds Trinity Church

He claimed solvent abuse and butane gas inhalation was going on under
the noses of residents.
Isle of Wight County Press

Ireland has become a major international base for large-scale peddling of
hard rugs.
Irish Press

Now coming onto the field to entertain the fans is the Air Force Academy
Drug and Bugle Corps.
Larry King, US TV football

Britain's leading shot putter pushed ahead from 18.33 metres in the dopening round to 18.47 in the fourth.
The Guardian

On Irish long jumper Jonathan Kron's drug ban for taking an illegal pain killer:
He took the substance innocently days before competing for an injured knee.
Christy Wall, Irish team official
(1995)

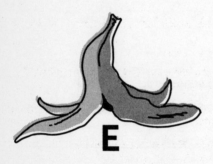

E

ECONOMIC FLAWCAST

We shall have no coal industry if the miners are driven into the ground.
Claire Brooks

British Rail stabbed us in the back by blowing the talks out of the water before they even got off the ground.
Jimmy Knapp

The free-enterprise system is absolutely too important to be left to the voluntary action of the marketplace.
Richard Kelly

What is the use of all these countries sending us aid, and then below the table kicking us in the teeth.
Anon. Thai politician

ESCAPE ACT

Three boys escaped when a wall collapsed at the Zoological Gardens, Regent's Park, London.
The Times

Yannick Noah always beats Kevin Curren. He has a sort of Houdini against him.
David Lloyd, BBC TV tennis

ETHNIC CLEANSING

I stand for anti-bigotry, anti-Semitism, anti-racism. That is what drives me.
**President George Bush
(1988)**

I can't change the apartheid laws back home [in South Africa]. *All I can do is call a spade a spade.*
Gerrie Coetzee

I'm not against blacks and a lot of the good blacks will attest to that.
Governor Evan Meechan of Arizona

That's a case of John Barnes doing the spadework for Luther Blissett.
John Motson, BBC TV football

He seems to have found a chink in Michael Chang's armour.
David Mercer

On a Chinese Olympic high-jumper:
There was a chink in Zhu's armour.
**David Coleman, BBC TV athletics
(1984)**

On a state visit to the USA:
Emperor Hirohito rides in an open carriage to Williamsburg. And our weatherman, Bob Kudzma says "There's a nip in the air."
**KDKA-TV
(1976)**

I ain't gonna let no darkies and white folks segregate together in this town.
**Eugene Connor, Police Commissioner, Birmingham, Alabama
(1950)**

To an Afro-American Democratic Party meeting:
My heart is as black as yours.
**Mario Procaccino
(1969)**

Equity Blacks 'Othello'.
***Daily Telegraph* headline**

The question of South Africa has been the nigger in the woodpile.
Ken Turner
(1982)

EXPLETIVE DELIGHTED

Swearing at the polo club? It's a load of bollocks!
Major Ronald Ferguson, father of the Duchess of York
(1987)

Paul Warhurst was sent off for foul and abusive language, but the lad swears blind he didn't say a word.
Joe Royle
(1990)

You won't find a single four-letter word in my autobiography. I don't go in for that bullshit.
Bob Feller

Famous midsouth resorts include Pinehurst and Southern Pines, where it is said that there are more golf curses per square mile than anywhere else in the world
North Carolina tourist brochure

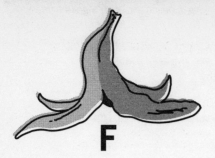

F

FAIR WELL

I'm here to say goodbye. Maybe not goodbye, but farewell.
Bobby Robson
(1990)

On the most requested songs of the week:
Sound Off is still on top, and I'd Like to Kiss You Goodnight on the bottom.
Anon. Australian DJ

FAN-TASTIC

Fifty-two thousand people here at Maine Road tonight, but my goodness, it seems like 50,000.
Bryon Butler, BBC Radio football

There's only 3000 people here tonight, and they're making enough noise for 4000.
Harry Carpenter, BBC TV boxing

Houston has its largest crowd of the night here this evening.
Jerry Coleman, US TV baseball

It was the sort of football game that would bring the crowds in any Saturday of the week.
Wally Barnes
(1974)

The crowd are literally electrified and glued to their seats.
Ted Lowe, BBC TV snooker
(1980)

I only hope people will come along in peace and enjoy a good fight.
Mickey Duff, BBC Radio 4
(1988)

You can almost hear the crowd's audible sigh of relief.
Bill McClaren, BBC TV rugby
(1979)

And the crowd are encouraging referee Thomas to blow his watch.
Hugh Johns, ITV football
(1974)

If the people don't want to come out to the ballpark, nobody's gonna stop them.
Lawrence 'Yogi' Berra

There is a commotion in the stands. I think it has something to do with a fat lady ... I've just been informed that the fat lady is the Queen of Holland.
Jay 'Dizzy' Dean, US TV baseball

FARMACY

The Americans have sowed the seed, and now they have reaped the whirlwind.
Sebastian Coe

If this debate is going to develop into one of general agricultural policy, I will have to ask permission to be allowed to speak again in order to cover a wider field.
Mr Belton

FEEL THE WIDTH

The East Germans are knitting well.
David Sanders, BBC TV cycling
(1976)

Goldline Upholstery Ltd. require an experienced upholsterer to cover the London and Kent area.
Buckingham Star
(1994)

FENCY FOOTWORK

I don't want to sit on the fence, but it could go either way.
Maurice Bamford

Don't sit on the fence, Terry. What chance do you think Germany has got of getting through?
Jimmy Hill
I think it's 50-50.
Terry Venables, BBC TV football

FINAL FRONTIER

Astronaut Alan Shephard is just beginning the final run through of his chick-list.
ABC TV

I have just learned that we do have film of the astronaut's breakfast, which should be coming up shortly.
Frank McGee, NBC TV News

The crew of the shuttle Discovery ... was going into medical isolation this afternoon after meeting President Reagan at the Johnson Space Centre.
Yorkshire Evening Post

You couldn't get me on Mars if it were the last place on earth.
Erma Cohen

Inside the Guild Hall was a Martian Arts Exhibition.
Western Evening Herald

I am convinced that UFOs exist, because I have seen one.
President Jimmy Carter
(1976)

On his UFO society :
Ours is a nuts and bolts organization.
Lionel Beer, *Spacelink*

FIRE FRIGHTERS

Bus On Fire - Passengers Alight.
West Wales Guardian headline

Salman Rushdie was playing with fire, sailing close to the wind and sticking his neck out.
Toby Jessel, BBC TV

Following the ceremony, a small reception was staged around a fire on the beach where the guests toasted the happy couple.
Forfar Courier

Manchester United are looking to Frank Stapleton to pull some magic out of the fire.
Jimmy Hill

They were torn between two fires.
US Congressman John Dent

FLAG DAY

The new Irish flag would be orange and green, and would in future be known as the Irish tricolour.
William Smith O'Brien

Our athletes are flying the flagship for British sport.
Fatima Whitbread

If Berger gets another yellow flag, it will be a red one.
David Coleman, BBC TV athletics
(1992)

Michael Heseltine should come out of the woodwork, stop waving his plastic chickens about, run up his flag up the flagpole and see who salutes.
John Banham
(1990)

FLASH POINT

It was observed that, at this particular crossing, in nearly every case, the time allowed for crossing was adequate, but there was great anxiety when the Green Man started flashing.
Hounslow Borough Engineer's report

We got people exposing themselves more in the summer. In winter it tends to drop off.
P.C. Andy Holden
(1995)

On the US Presidential race :
Richard Nixon has been sitting in the White House, while George McGovern has been exposing himself to the people of the United States.
Governor Frank Licht of Rhode Island (1972)

Topless Bar - £1 cover charge.
Sign in Soho

Well, the streakers are at it again. This time at a local football game just outside of Boston. I can't figure out this type of behaviour - I guess it's their way of showing they're nuts.
Larry Glick, WBZ Radio (Boston)

While others are waiting please remove your clothes as soon as the light goes out.
Sign in Norfolk launderette

Six girls struggled from sick beds on Tuesday for a last-minute rehearsal for the final ceremony and downed their swimsuits.
Singapore Times

Nudists May Get Coastal Strip.
Anon. Sussex newspaper headline

Pretty Maids All In A Row directed by Roger Vadim, the man who uncovered Brigitte Bardot and Jane Fonda.
Wilson Hatcher, Channel 41 (Louisville)

FLOOD WARNING

When shall the lion of autocracy walk hand in hand with the floodgates of democracy?
James Sexton MP

From his emergency flood HQ at City Hall, Mayor Friedman has just ordered all families living near or adjacent to the Mill River to ejaculate immediately
Dave Duncan, Radio WKLW (Rhode Island)

FLOWER POWER

Send mother a gift of hardly ever blooming rose bushes.
Sioux Falls Argus Leader

Body In Garden Was A Plant, Says Wife.
***Morning Post* headline**

Bristol Flower Group Pick Their Leader.
Bristol Evening Post headline

It will create an excitement that will sweep the country like wildflowers.
Samuel Goldwyn

FOOD FOR FAULT

You'd better cut my pizza into four slices, I don't think I can eat eight.
Lawrence 'Yogi' Berra

Boycott, somewhat a creature of habit, likes exactly the sort of food he himself prefers.
Don Mosey, BBC Radio cricket

On television cookery with the Craddocks:
Let's hope your doughnuts come out like Fanny's.
Frank Bough, BBC TV

Would the Minister say whether the bakers who supply the Army and the public authorities use yeast and salt, and fuel and petrol?
General Richard Mulcahy

I'll have pie à la mode with cream.
Johnny Logan

You can't have your pound of flesh and eat it too.
William Deedes

You can't make an omelette without frying eggs.
William Deedes

If we think they will be easy meat we'll end up with egg on our faces.
Terry Dolan
(1989)

It's a case of putting all our eggs into the next 90 minutes.
Phil Neal

Dudley Moore without a piano is like chalk without cheese.
Nick Owen

Nothing comes close to boxing. It should be added to the list: chocolate, champagne, sex.
Chris Eubank

It's a political hot potato around their necks.
Dr. Marks

It depends on whether there are any more hot potatoes waiting to come over the horizon.
William Waddell

He went down like a sack of potatoes, then made a meal of it.
Trevor Brooking, BBC football

He's the one rotten apple who turns out to be the good egg.
William Feaver

Party will leave bus station and alight at Highcliffe. Tea at Barton-on-Sea. Small chisels advised.
Natural Science Society Programme

The female teachers were instructed in cooking. They had, in fact, to go through the process of cooking themselves.
Report by Commissioners of National Education in Ireland

The restaurant is now open Friday and Saturday nights for à la carte and Sunday lunch.
Hastings Observer

Ex-Boxer Battered Outside Chip Shop.
Cheltenham Echo
(1979)

Black Dog Inn. If you eat here you won't get better.
Blackmore Vale Magazine advert

Toot Shors' restaurant is so crowded nobody goes there any more.
Lawrence 'Yogi' Berra

In Japan, I suppose apples are small bananas compared to rice.
Rhod Sharp, BBC Radio 5
(1995)

Do you think I came up the Clyde on a banana skin?
Robin Charters

Seven eggs were hurled at the President's car. He ducked as three smashed into the windscreen of his pullet-proof limousine.
Daily Express

Dinner: 4oz braised lover (cooked with beef stock cube).
Scotland Sunday Standard

Come and try our Greek special ties at a famous restaurant.
Anon. food guide

FOOLS RUSH IN

I don't seem to use my intelligence intelligently.
Virginia Wade
(1977)

I know a lot of people think I'm dumb. Well, at least, I ain't no educated fool.
Leon Spinks

We're more aggressive, more mobile, and more smarter.
Greg Lloyd

I've always been a bit more maturer than what I am.
Samantha Fox

I'm going to graduate on time, no matter how long it takes.
Rod Brooken

We're going to have the best educated Americans in the world.
Vice President Dan Quayle

Quite frankly, teachers are the only profession that teaches our children.
Vice President Dan Quayle

FOOT WHERE?

I wouldn't like to be sitting in Alain Prost's shoes right now.
Barry Sheene
(1989)

You can bet your boots if the shoe was on the other foot the Americans wouldn't wear it.
Sandra Dickinson

I've got ten pairs of training shoes, one for each day of the week.
Samantha Fox

At the fair they were exhibiting a full range of shoes for girls with low-cut fancy uppers.
Leicester Mercury

Goodbye my dear chap and remember ... don't burn your boots.
William Deedes

FOREIGN TONGUE

Sunderland are suffering from déjà vu - a case of 'what will be, will be'.
Lennie Lawrence, ITV Football

It's déjà vu all over again.
Lawrence 'Yogi' Berra

Johann Cruyff, at the age of 35, added a whole new meaning to the word 'anno Domini'.
Archie MacPherson, BBC TV football

You'd better caveat that statement.
Alexander Haig, US Secretary of State

'Numero Eins' - as they say in Germany.
Peter Jones, BBC Radio football

If Don Mattingly isn't the American League MVP, nothing in China is kosher.
Phil Rizutto

Hey listen. I'm a member of the National Rifle Association. You're hurting my feelings, as they say in China.
President George Bush

There's nothing like seeing two protagonists having a nose-to-nose tête-à-tête.
Richard Skinner

FREE DUMB

I believe we are on irreversible trend towards more freedom and democracy. But that could change.
Vice President Dan Quayle

We must believe in free will. We have no choice.
Isaac Bashevis Singer, novelist

That's part of American greatness - discrimination. Yes sir, inequality breeds freedom and gives a man opportunity.
Governor Lester Maddox of Georgia

FOR SALE

For sale: Elizabethan cassette recorder, as new.
£11.50.
Salcombe Gazette

For sale: 100 year-old brass bed. Perfect for antique lover.
Evening Star

For sale: To a kind master, full grown, domesticated tigress, goes
daily walk untied, and eats flesh from hand.
Calcutta Express

For sale: Nappies used by two babies. £5 for 2 dozen.
Kingston Informer

For sale: Phillips ultra-violent lamp.
Watford Evening Echo

For sale: Delightful kittens. House-trained after four o'clock phone
Worthing XXXXXX.
West Sussex newspaper

For sale: Gents' skirts 16" collar.
Glasgow Evening Times

For sale: Wedding dress, size 10, ejaculate condition.
Worthing Trader

For sale: Rosewood piano, owner going abroad with beautiful
twisted legs.
North Wales Advertiser

For sale: Antique piano with candelabra and spiral staircase.
Edinburgh Advertiser

For sale: Small electric organ, good for learning £30 ono. Also
large orgasm.
Wandsworth Times

For sale: Hotpoint Supermatic twin-tub. Good education.
Edinburgh Evening News

For sale: Gobbling Tea Maid with alarm. £12.
Derby Evening Telegraph

For sale: 18 cwt solitaire engagement ring. £80 ono.
Bristol Evening Post

For sale: Complete mahogany Chip & Dale dining room set.
Long Island Press

For sale: Six million dollar man £3.
Worcester Source

For sale: Large crystal vase by lady slightly cracked.
Long Island Press

For sale: 1928 Rolls-Royce hearse. Original body.
The Times

For sale: Ford Granada hearse with new body.
Irish Press

For sale: 1983 Ford Grandad.
Wolverhampton Express and Star

For sale: 1978 Fish van with scales £600.
Evening Gazette

For sale: Amazing offer. Fish and chip fryer made from chip-resistant enamel.
Dalton's Weekly

For sale: Phillips fish washer. 12 place setting. £50.
Stirling News

For sale: Hammers - bulk purchase. Suit some handymen with claw heads.
Petersfield Post

For sale: Bath. Late Victorian as used by chartered accountant with clawed feet.
Hampstead and Highgate Express

Craft workers sell your gods at Charing Cross Methodist Church fair.
**North Wales Quids-In
(1995)**

Free cholesterol testing will be offered at 10 this morning. The cost is $6.
Hammond, Indiana Times

FULL BACKING

Welsh rugby union chiefs gave their full backing to a judge after he jailed a violent player who stamped on an opponent's head for six months.
**Daily Post
(1994)**

All the Leeds United team are 100 per cent behind the manager, but I can't speak for the rest of the squad.
**Brian Greenhoff
(1980)**

Bobby Gould thinks I'm trying to stab him in the back. In fact I'm right behind him.
**Stuart Pearson
(1992)**

Gentlemen, a member of this House had taken advantage of my absence to tweak my nose behind my back. I hope that the next time he abuses me behind my back like a coward he will do it to my face like a man, and not go skulking into the thicket to assail a gentleman who isn't present to defend himself.
Anon. Australian MP

FUTURE SPEAK

Some names to look forward to ... perhaps in the future.
David Coleman, BBC TV sport

Things happen more frequently in the future than they do in the past.
Governor Booth Gardner of Washington

On writing for TV's 'Star Trek':
I'm interested in stories about people as we know them in the near-recent future.
Philip Kaufman

It's a question of whether we're going to forward into the future, or past to the back.
Vice President Dan Quayle

(This gaffe has also been seen reported in the following form: The question is, whether we are going forward to tomorrow or we're going to go past in the back.)

Most of our future lies ahead.
Denny Crum

I've seen the future and it's pretty much like the present, only longer.
Dan Quisenberry

We should not look at the immediate situation in terms of planning a new move in any time-frame that is now immediately foreseeable.
Henry Kissinger, US Secretary of State

Rest of the year may not follow January.
***Wall Street Journal* headline**

G

GLOBALONEY

I've been batting all over the world ... and in other countries too.
Keith Miller, ABC TV
(1982)

The United States is at peace with all the world, and sustains friendly relations with the rest of mankind.
President Benjamin Harrison

The World Cup ... truly an international event.
John Motson, BBC TV World Cup football

The Embassy ... the world championships of the world.
Tony Green, BBC TV darts
(1996)

GOLF CLUBBED

Winners of the mixed gruesomes at the Strawberry Hill Golf Club were Mrs M. Steward and N. Ince with 34 points.
Richmond Times

He was advised by his local caddie to take a two iron, settled instead for a tree and smashed the ball 220 yards straight into the hole.
Bristol Evening Post

GLOVE STORY

Perhaps boxing could be made safer if gloves were heavier.
Judge James Pickles
(1995)

The dumbest question I was ever asked by a sportswriter was whether I hit harder with red or white gloves. As a matter of fact, I hit harder with red.
Frank Crawford

The clay feet of Germany will be revealed when we take off the gloves.
Letter to Sunday Chronicle
(1914)

GRAVE NEWS

I say that if Lincoln were alive today he would turn over in his grave.
President Gerald Ford

At President Pompidou's funeral in Paris :
This is a great day for France.
President Richard Nixon
(1974)

Leningrad must be spinning in his grave.
Don King
(1987)

Efforts are being made in New York to stop undertakers charging the earth for burials.
Daily Telegraph

Always go to other people's funerals, otherwise they won't come to yours.
Lawrence 'Yogi' Berra

A family of three were seriously ill in hospital last night after being found unconscious by their dead dog.
Sunday People

She has visited the cemetery where her husband was buried on a number of occasions.
Shropshire Star

I wouldn't believe Adolf Hitler was dead, even if he told me so himself.
Hjalmar Schacht, German financier

New York Ban On Boxing After Death.
The Times headline

Even when you're dead, you must never allow yourself just to lie and be buried.
Gordon Lee

The Phillies beat the Cubs today in a double-header. That puts another keg in the Cubs' coffin.
Jerry Coleman, US TV baseball

That was the nail that broke the coffin's back.
Jack Kraft

A microwave oven has been stolen from Weeley Crematorium, police said yesterday.
East Anglian Daily Times

GRATE BRITAIN

We are not wholly an island, except geographically.
John Major, Prime Minister

And the next request is from a listener who lives in Bury Street, Edmunds, in Suffolk.
Johnny Walker, BBC Radio 1

A truly international field, no Britons involved.
David Coleman, BBC Radio athletics

SAM GOLDWYN
(1882-1974)

Polish-born Hollywood producer Samuel Goldfish changed his name and almost changed the course of the English language. Unlike any other international gaffer Sam Goldwyn spoon-fed many of his prize gaffes to the public via the services of his film studio's press officers, who made up a great many of the more celebrated Goldwynisms.

The passage of time has drawn a dusty veil over which utterings were real and which were manufactured, either way they both make great reading.

I never liked you, and I always will.

Include me out.

Don't talk to me while I'm interrupting.

Modern dancing is so old-fashioned.

It's more than magnificent - it's mediocre.

Sex will outlive us all.

The scene is too dull. Tell him to put more life into his dying.

This makes me so sore, it got my dandruff up.

If I entered into an agreement with that man, I would be sticking my head in a moose.

I am willing to admit that I may not always be right, but I am never wrong.

This will start with a bang in Hollywood and degenerate throughout the whole world.

Spare no expense to make everything as economical as possible.

You've got to take the sour with the bitter.

Don't pay any attention to the critics ... don't even ignore them.

If you don't disagree with me, how will I know I'm right?

The trouble with the movie business is the dearth of bad pictures.

I go to the movies every night of the week. I've got to do something to take my mind off business.

I want this to be 50-50 like I said, but I want you to make sure I get the best part of it.

Gentlemen, listen to me more slowly.

You don't realize what life's all about until you have found yourself lying on the brink of a great abscess.

Keep up a stiff upper chin.

Go see this picture to see for yourself why you shouldn't go and see it.

I don't think anyone should write his autobiography until after he's dead.

When told there were only 12 disciples in his film The Last Supper:
Only 12? Well go out and get me thousands!

When told how a sun-dial works:
What will they think of next.

Our comedies are not to be laughed at.

Here I am paying big money to you writers and what for? All you do is change the words.

For your information, I'd like to ask a question.

A verbal contract isn't worth the paper it is written on.

In two words - Im Possible.

GRAMMER SKOOL
(US grade school howlers)

The parts of speech are air and lungs.

The people who live in Moscow are known as Mosquitoes.

A census taker is the man who goes from home to home increasing the population.

Water is composed of two gins - oxygin and hydrogin. Oxygin is pure gin, while hydrogin is gin and water.

H_2O = hot water. CO_2 = cold water.

A virgin forest is a forest where the hand of man has never set foot.

Most of the homes in France are made of plaster of Paris.

The spinal cord is a long bunch of bones. The head sits on the top and you sit on the bottom.

A scout obeys all to whom obedience is due and respects all duly constipated authorities.

The four seasons are salt, pepper, vinegar and mustard.

The word trousers is an uncommon noun because it is singular at the top and plural at the bottom.

Syntax is the money collected in church from sinners.

Steel was discovered because someone smelt it.

Frederic Handel was half English, half German and half Italian. He was rather large.

J.S. Bach died from 1750 to the present day.

Beethoven was so deaf that he wrote loud music.

Most composers do not live until they are dead.

Music sung by two people at the same time is called a duel.

Most authorities agree that music of antiquity was written long ago.

Both of the Aston Villa scorers, Withe and Mortimer, were born in Liverpool, as was Villa manager, Ron Saunders, who was born in Birkenhead.
David Coleman, BBC TV football

Chesterfield 1, Chester 1. Another score draw there in that local derby.
Desmond Lynam, Grandstand, BBC TV

On the outline map of England and Wales provided, shade in the Highlands of Scotland.
Lancashire and Cheshire Schools Examination Question

Liverpool St Station, the greatest development in London since the Great Fire of 1666.
Guy Michelmore

It is no further from the north coast of Spitsbergen to the North Pole than it is from Land's End to John of Gaunt.
Rev. William Spooner

GRAVESTONED

Erected in memory of John Philips accidentally shot
As a mark of respect by his brother.
Anon. gravestone

GROUND IMPROVEMENTS

For those of you who know the Selhurst Park Ground, West Ham are playing from right to left.
Anon. radio commentator

The Queen's Park Oval, exactly as its name suggests, absolutely round.
Tony Cozier, BBC Radio cricket

When Stoke unveiled their floodlights in 1956 they asked Port Vale to do the honours with a match.
The Guardian

Many supporters say they wouldn't stand for all-seater stadiums.
Guy Michelmore

I try to tell our guys that the altitude isn't that bad because we're playing indoors.
Jerry Tarkanian

GUN SMOKE

On Sarah Jane Moore's failed attempt to assassinate President Ford :
*There are too many guns in the hands of people who don't know how to
use them.*
Former Vice President Hubert H. Humphrey

The big guns haven't pulled out all the stops yet.
David Coleman, BBC TV athletics

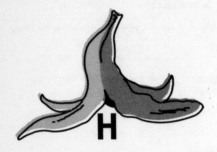

HALF-MAN

Ron Guidry is not very big, maybe 140 pounds, but he has an arm like a lion.
Jerry Coleman, US TV baseball

Gonzo leaps like a giraffe and grabs it.
Jerry Coleman, US TV baseball

This man could be a dark horse.
David Coleman, BBC TV athletics

HAPPY, HAPPY TALK

Earl Weaver is not happy unless he's not happy.
Elrod Hendricks

I like playing in Sheffield, it's full of melancholy happy-go-lucky people.
Alex Higgins

HAT TRICK

They're hanging on to their hats for grim life.
Eve Pollard

Princess Margaret ... wearing an off-the-hat face.
Max Robertson, BBC Radio

John Curry is appearing in the play, but he's not wearing his skates - he's got a completely different hat on his head this time.
Peter Levy

HISTORY LESSENS

History is all about todays and not about yesterdays.
Brian Moore, ITV football

I do not intend to prejudge the past.
William Whitelaw MP
(1972)

If history repeats itself, I should think we can expect the same thing again.
Terry Venables, BBC TV football

As King Henry VIII said to each of his three wives, "I won't keep you long".
President Ronald Reagan

This is the greatest heap of bulldust since Marx first enunciated his Mein Kampf or whatever it was.
Sir Magnus Cormack
(1978)

If you think of the other hostages, you take Terry Waite and Paul McCartney - their families have behaved impeccably.
Sir John Stokes

The visiting lecturer next week will be Professor Hugh Trevor Roper, well-known for his research on Adolf Hitler who will talk about Sir Walter Scott.
Yorkshire Post

It is indeed fitting that we gather here today to pay tribute to Abraham Lincoln, who was born in a log cabin that he built with his own hands.
Anon. US senator
(This is a much used Ronald Reagan joke.)

After winning the F.A. Cup:
Few teams in the history of football can have leapt to fame as rapidly as Sunderland. The Club was founded in 1879.
F.A. Year Book
(1973)

It's like the Roman Empire. Everybody running around covered with syphilis. And then it was destroyed by a volcano.
Joan Collins, *Playboy*
(1984)

The Pope's visit to Canterbury in May will be the greatest Roman Catholic occasion in this country since the Reformation.
Kent Messenger

Rome wasn't burned in a day.
Abe Hirschfield

We need to go into our next match with all guns blazing - like the Charge of the Light Brigade.
Andy Roxburgh
(1991)

There's more ice down here than sunk the Bismarck.
Gerry Francis
(1991)

Even Napoleon had his Watergate.
Lawrence 'Yogi' Berra

The skeleton was believed to be that of a Saxon worrier.
Express and Echo

On the Nazi holocaust :
It was an obscene period in our nation's history ... no, not in our nation's but in World War Two. We all lived in this century, I didn't live in this century but in this century's history.
Vice President Dan Quayle

And for those of you who don't know Australia House, it's a beautiful Victorian building. The first brick was laid in 1913 by King George V.
Rolf Harris

HORNS OF A DILEMMA

Someone in the England team will have to grab the ball by the horns.
Ron Atkinson, ITV football
(1993)

Since the government has let the cat out of the bag there is nothing else to do but take the bull by the horns.
Jeremiah MacVeagh MP

She has got to take her nerves by the horns.
Virginia Wade, BBC tennis

HORSE SENSE

Red Rum is in a stable condition.
Anon. newsreader, BBC Radio 5
(1992)

Hark! I hear a white horse coming.
Dialogue from *The Lone Ranger* US radio show

Celtic Swing, the biggest talking horse of the summer.
Angus Loughran, Channel One TV
(1995)

Secretariat is only human.
Steve Pinkus

This horse has had a lot of foot trouble, that has dogged him throughout his career.
John Pitman, BBC TV horse racing
(1995)

We've had a tip [for the 1994 Epsom Derby] here in the studio for a horse called Colonel Collins. Now I don't know much about horse-racing, but I believe he won the race last year.
Anon presenter, Jersey Radio
(1994)
(Horses can only run in one Epsom Derby.)

Deputy O'Reilly was put up as a stalking horse. And he came in here and made a complete ass of himself.
James M. Dillon

These two horses have met five times this season, and they've beaten each other on each occasion.
Jimmy Linley, BBC TV horse racing

The press is still barking on a dead horse.
Alan Croxford
(1982)

And now coming to the rider jump there's a waterless horse in front.
Raymond Glendenning

Nigel Havers and I hit it off like a horse on fire.
Tony Britton

The American horses know the fences like the back of their hand.
Harvey Smith

A HOUSE IS NOT A HOME

Try a flat or a maisonette, they are the ultimate inconvenience.
Solihull Times

*There is no housing shortage in Lincoln today, just a rumour that is put
about by people who have nowhere to live.*
Mayor G. L. Marfin of Lincoln

*Buying or selling a house could cost you dear. See a Solicitor, just to be
sure.*
***Yorkshire Evening Post* advert**

HOW LONG

*We estimate, and this isn't an estimation, that Greta Waitz is 80 seconds
behind.*
David Coleman, BBC TV athletics

*He is accelerating all the time. This last lap was run in 64 seconds and
the one before that in 62 seconds.*
David Coleman, BBC TV athletics

Liverpool aren't getting forward as they were in the early first five minutes.
Bryan Hamilton, BBC Radio 5
(1995)

*Merseyside derbies usually last 90 minutes and I'm sure today's won't be
any different.*
Trevor Brooking, BBC TV football

Hodge scored for Forest after only 22 seconds, totally against the run of play.
Peter Lorenzo, ITV football

Arsenal now have plenty of time to dictate these last few seconds.
Peter Jones - BBC Radio Football

Seventeen minutes gone and already no goals.
Ron Jones

Thirteen minutes before the end, talk about a last-minute goal.
Simon Mayo, BBC Radio

We actually got the winner with three minutes to go, but then they equalized.
Ian McNail

A preview of comedy-adventure films will be featured at the library on Tuesday. The one hour programme lasts about one hour and 45 minutes.
Newhall Signal and Saugus Enterprise

The first 90 minutes [in a football match] are the most important.
Bryan Robson

An equalizer here could lead to a level score after 90 minutes.
Elton Welsby, ITV football

There are no opportune times for a penalty, and this is not one of them.
Jack Youngblood, NBC TV, US football

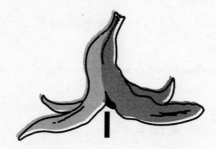

IN-DIRECTION

The nearest hotel was five miles away in one direction and practically 12 miles in the opposite direction.
Irish Ulster Magazine

Carl Lewis, what a great runner. All his arms and elbows and knees running in the same direction.
**Anon. BBC Radio 5 athletics commentator
(1992)**

INJURY TIME

Graves is likely to be out for a month with a broken index finger on his bottom hand.
Robin Marlar, *Sunday Times*
(1978)

[James] Bond's knees, the Achilles heel of all skiers, were beginning to ache.
Ian Fleming

And as so often with the Achilles tendon injuries, the Achilles goes.
Pat Pocock

That type of injury could permanently hurt a batter for a long time.
Pete Rose

Daley Thompson, not the most open of athletes, has been keeping the condition of his leg injury close to his chest.
Daily Telegraph

The Stoke City defender has knee and thing injuries.
The Guardian
(1976)

Bruce Benedict may not be hurt as much as he really is.
Jerry Coleman, US TV baseball

From the way Denny's shaking his head, he's either got an injured shoulder or a gnat in his eye.
Jerry Coleman, US TV baseball

There's nothing wrong with his shoulder except some pain - and pain doesn't hurt you.
Sparky Anderson
(1989)

He's got to go in for a hernia operation, but when he gets over that he'll be back in harness again.
Peter Alliss, BBC TV golf
(1988)

I'm afraid that Francis has been suffering from a panacea of injury.
Dale Barnes

My goals are to hit 300, score 100 runs and stay injury prone.
Mickey Rivers

Peter Weir has just shrugged off an ankle injury.
Jock Brown

Gus Logie sustained a broken nose during net practice ... bit by a ball

from Colin Croft.
Daily Telegraph

And there's Kevin Ward raising his crutch to the fans.
Ray French, Sky TV rugby
(1993)

Dag-Otto Lauritzen, who took up cycling as therapy after injuring his leg in a parachute accident, jumped in at the deep end in yesterday's stage of the Kellogg Tour from Newport.
The Guardian

Steve McCahill has limped off with a badly cut forehead.
Tom Ferrie

Shaun Edwards has happy memories of Wembley. On his last appearance here he received a fractured cheek-bone.
Ray French, BBC TV rugby

And he's got the icepack on his groin there, so possibly not the old shoulder injury.
Ray French, Sky TV rugby

I've never had major knee surgery on any other part of my body.
Winston Bennett

You'll be hoping that this run of injuries will stop earlier than it started.
Andrew Gidley

And Steve Cram's ankle injury is another headache the selectors could do without.
Anon. athletics commentator, GWR Radio

He's recovered from a calf injury, but is back in the fold now.
John Helm, SportsWire TV football
(1994)

This is the first injury of the match ... which is a great joy.
Bill Maclaren, BBC TV rugby
(1994)

Sure there have been injuries and deaths in boxing, but none of them serious.
Alan Minter

After his fall, Carl Llewellyn is OK. He's just walked into the ambulance.
Peter O'Sullevan, BBC TV horse racing
(1994)

A brain scan has revealed Andrew Caddick is not suffering from a stress fracture of the shin.
Jo Sheldon

INSURANCE CLAIMS

Coming home I drove into the wrong house and collided with a tree I don't have.

The other car collided with mine without giving warning of its intent.

I collided with a stationary truck coming the other way.

In my attempt to kill a fly, I drove into a telegraph pole.

I had been shopping for plants all day and was on my way home. As I reached an intersection, a hedge sprang up, obscuring my vision and I did not see the other car.

I had been driving for 40 years when I fell asleep at the wheel and had an accident.

I was on my way to the doctor with rear end trouble when my universal joint gave way causing me to have an accident.

My car was legally parked as it backed into the other vehicle.

As I approached the intersection, a sign suddenly appeared in a place where no sign had ever appeared before, making me unable to avoid the accident.

I told the police I was not injured, but upon removing my hair I found that I had a fractured skull.

I was sure the other fellow would never make it to the other side of the road when I struck him.

I saw a slow-moving, sad-faced old gentleman as he bounced off the hood of my car.

The indirect cause of the accident was a little guy in a small car with a big mouth.

I was thrown from my car as it left the road

and was later found in a ditch by some stray cows.

A pedestrian hit me and went under my car.

I thought my window was down, but I found out it was up when I put my head through it.

To avoid hitting the bumper of the car in front, I struck the pedestrian.

The guy was all over the road. I had to swerve a number of times before I hit him.

The pedestrian had no idea which way to run, so I ran over him.

An invisible car came out of nowhere, struck my car and vanished.

A truck backed through my windshield into my wife's face.

I pulled away from the side of the road, glanced at my mother-in-law, and headed over the embankment.

When asked about his knee injury:
It's the sort of thing you take on the chin.
**Va'iga Tuigamala
(1995)**

I thought he was going to dive and decapitate himself, badly.
Mike Hendrick, BBC TV cricket

Now the trainer has been called on to the pitch ... and he's having to administer artificial insemination.
Anon. radio commentator

INSECT BITES

As the caterpillar approaches the larva stage it becomes more sluggish.
Anon. presenter, Channel 4 TV

The 75 year-old hotel closed for the last time after housing a number of businesses and ten ants.
Boise Idaho Statesman

Enkalon is to get £1,500,000 via the Northern Ireland Office to keep the textiles and carpet yarn factory open for another seven moths.
Daily Telegraph

INTEREST STING

I'll tell you one fact - it may be boring but it's interesting.
Barbara Cartland

I find it interesting how we carried away by the dogma à la mode.
Lincoln Diaz-Ballart

IN THE FRAME

Jawbone of an ass! Never, in one of my pictures! We will use the whole ass!
Cecil B. de Mille

Replying to director Franco Zeffirelli confirming their over-budget film Jesus of Nazareth had 12 disciples in it:
Twelve! Who needs 12? Couldn't we make do with six?
Lew Grade

When asked if he wanted a powerful speech like Hamlet's soliloquy:
No! I want something like that "To be or not to be be..."
Harry Cohn

She's got talent and personality. Just give me two years, and I'll make her an instant overnight star.
Harry Cohn

We won't make a sequel to Batman, but we may well make a second episode.
Jon Peters

IRON LADY

What Mrs Thatcher's closest friends are wondering is whether ... she is beginning to suffer from metal fatigue.
The Guardian

The Thatcher household did not spend 24 hours a day discussing politics over the early morning tea.
Carol Thatcher, daughter of Margaret Thatcher

J

JAM TODAY

Traffic is very heavy at the moment, so if you are thinking of leaving now, you'd better set off of a few minutes earlier.
Anon. A.A. radio announcer

JEST MY IMAGINATION

I imagine that the conditions in those cars today are totally unimaginable.
Murray Walker, BBC TV motor racing

I can't imagine what kind of problem Senna has. I imagine it must be some kind of grip problem.
Murray Walker, BBC TV motor racing

JEUX SANS FRONTIERES

If you can't make the putts and can't get the man in from second base in the bottom of the ninth, you're not going to win enough football games in this league, and that's the problem we had today.
Sam Rutigliano, US football TV commentator

Sir Peter Parker played the final card in what's been a tricky game of chess.
John Perkins

It's like a game of chess: all the cards are thrown in the air, the board's turned over and you're in a whole new ball game.
Michael Howard MP

It is unfortunate that Watergate happened, but people are using it as a political football to bury my brother.
Donald Nixon

Cricket shouldn't be used as a political football.
David Graveney

I think you'll see some improvement as we get better.
Anon. US football coach

The run of the ball is not always in our court at the moment.
Phil Neal

On the Falklands War:
This is the run-up to the big match which should be a walk-over.
**Rear Admiral Sandy Woodward
(1982)**

JOBLESSE OBLIGE

British unemployment is rising faster here than in any other European country.
Neil Kinnock MP

The interests of the employers and the employed are the same nine times out of ten. I will even say 99 times out of ten.
Lord Curzon

We have more people employed in this country than ever before. Sure unemployment is up, but more people are looking for work than ever before.
William Rusher

BRIAN JOHNSTON

Brian Johnston, or Johnners as he was lovingly known, was a man for whom every rainy day at a cricket ground always yielded its own particular ray of sunshine. He loved four things in life: a joke, a chocolate cake, a game of cricket and a verbal gaffe.

As *The Times* remembered in its obituary in 1994, *"He was a man whose personal church clock stood perpetually at 10 to 3, and for whom there was always honey for tea. Not just honey either: cream cake and sponge cake and cherry cake and Dundee cake and walnut cake ... Johnston's enduring contribution to Western civilisation is the cake-by-cake commentary".*

Many have thought that some of his faux pas were contrived and neatly slotted in where the occasion arose, but the following example proves that a man without an ounce of malice in his body was prone, live on air, to the most unfortunate of gaffes.

During the 1980 England v West Indies test match series:
Deryck Murray has batted well. He is the nigger in the woodpile as far as the English are concerned.

There's a small crowd here to watch this important game, in fact I would say there are more cars than people.

Play has ended here at Southampton, but they play until seven at Edgbaston, so over there now for some more balls from Rex Alston.

During a Middlesex v Sussex cricket match:
The latest news is that Warr's declared.

After the New Zealand batsman was dealt a painful blow to the box by the fifth delivery of an over:
Glenn Turner looks a bit shaky and unsteady, but I think he's going to bat on - one ball left.

Neil Harvey's at slip, with his legs wide apart, waiting for a tickle.

Fred Titmus has two short legs, one of them square.

You've come over at a very appropriate time; Ray Illingworth has just relieved himself at the pavilion end.

Perhaps Johnners's most famous slip of the tongue came as he welcomed viewers back to a 1976 Test match, as England batsman Peter Willey faced up to the West Indies fast bowler Michael Holding, *"The bowler's Holding, the batsman's Willey"*.

JUST SAY NO!

The referee was very positive. He said, "No!"
Tony Ricketts, SportsWire TV football
(1995)

I answer in the affirmative with an emphatic, "No!".
Sir Boyle Roche MP

The President doesn't want yes-men and yes-women around him. When he says no, we all say no.
Elizabeth Dole, US politician

K

KILL OR CURE

I don't believe in stopping fights. Even if a guy is getting too much of a beating. If he's done, let him be done ... it's just like a mercy killing.
Jake LaMotta

KINDRED SPIRITS

There's a lot of heredity in that family.
Ralph Kiner, US TV baseball

I owe a lot to my parents, especially my mother and father.
Greg Norman

I'd like to thank all my parents.
Julie Inskter

Both Annie Ross's Scottish parents were in the theatre and her mother is comedian Jimmy Logan.
Akhbar Oman

Here on Father's Day, we again wish you all happy birthday.
Ralph Kiner, US TV baseball

My sister's expecting a baby, and I don't know if I'm going to be an uncle or an aunt.
Chuck Nevitt

His brother failed, so let's see if he can succeed and maintain the family tradition.
David Coleman, BBC sport

Today is Reg Kray's birthday. Happy birthday Reg. Not sure when his twin brother Ronnie's is, but best wishes to Ron anyway.
Nicky Campbell

To Steve Albert:
Are you any relation to your brother, Marv?
Leon Wood

L

LANGUAGE BARRIER

Start your own language school. Very lucrative business. Knowledge of languages not necessary.
India Weekly

Every monumental inscription should be in Latin, for that being a dead language, it will ever live.
Samuel Johnson

There are so many Latino ball-players, we're going to have to get a Latin instructor up here.
Phil Rizutto, US TV baseball

LAVATORY HUMOUR

There is no toilet accommodation on the Alton part of the train. We apologize for this inconvenience.
British Rail (Waterloo) announcement

A chemical toilet has disappeared from Corton's pitch-and-putt course. Lowestoft police say they have nothing to go on.
Eastern Evening News

Over now to Nigel Starmer-Smith, who has had seven craps as scrum-half for England.
Jimmy Hill, BBC TV rugby

LAW-LESS

I haven't committed a crime. What I did was fail to comply with the law.
Mayor David Dinkins of New York

I can't think of any new law existing law that's in force that wasn't before.
President George Bush

I favour the irrigation bill in order that we may turn the barren hills of my state into fruitful valleys.
Anon. US senator

This legislation has far-reaching ramifications.
Glb Lewis

LIGHT FANTASTIC

Football's not like an electric light. You can't just flick the button and change from slow to quick.
John Greig

The light which the Lord Chancellor had thrown upon the matter was darkness.
Lord Ribblesdale

LIKE FOR LIKE

Glenn Hoddle hasn't been the Hoddle we know. Neither has Bryan Robson.
Ron Greenwood

They compare Steve McManaman to Steve Heighway and he's nothing like him, but I can see why - it's because he's a bit different.
Kevin Keegan

There's no way Ryan Giggs is another George Best. He's another Ryan Giggs.
Denis Law

The only thing I have in common with George Best is that we come from the same place ... play for the same club ... and were discovered by the same man.
Norman Whiteside

You can't compare Lennox Lewis to Muhammad Ali, but he's not dissimilar.
Gary Mason
(1992)

Mark Hughes, Sparky by name and sparky by nature, and the same can be said of Steve McMahon.
Brian Moore, ITV football

Not unlike it, but not very like it either.
Lord John Oaksey, Channel 4 Racing

A LITTLE KNOWLEDGE...

You never know when the end of a rainbow will cease.
Angelo Dundee
(1978)

I can't tell who is leading, it's either Oxford or Cambridge.
John Snagge, BBC TV boat race

On Jean Cocteau's *The Seashell and the Clergyman:*
The film is unquestionably meaningless, but if it has any meaning it is doubtless objectionable.
British Board of Film Censors

I don't know what's going on out there, but whatever it is it's diabolical.
Jimmy Greaves, ITV football
(1991)

LOAD OF BALLS

The band playing, people picnicking round the ground, while on the field

hundreds of small boys are playing with their balls.
Rex Alston, BBC cricket

Unprecedented Event: Undergraduates Scratch Balls.
***Oxford Mail** headline*

The only change England would propose might be to replace Derek Pringle, who remains troubled by no balls.
The Times

It is extremely cold here. The England fielders are keeping their hands in pockets between balls.
Christopher Martin-Jenkins, BBC Radio cricket

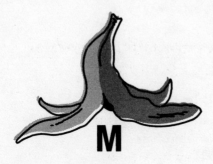

M

MAIL EGO

Direct mail ... it falls out of every magazine you open these days.
Derek Jameson

Remember, postcards only, please. The winner will be the first one opened.
Brian Moore, ITV football
(1977)

MEDIC AIL

Cheer up, it's a sunny day and we're talking about breast cancer.
Anon. presenter, Greater London Radio

The health of Mr Parnell has lately taken a very serious turn, and fears of his recovery are entertained by his friends.
Anon. 19th-century Irish newspaper

Mark Scratches after 'Mystery' Rash.
***The Times* headline
(1970)**

Several Vikings hit with intestinal infection: More colour photos, page 14c.
***Minneapolis Star Tribune* sports headline**

X-Rays of 'Dizzy' Dean's head show nothing.
Anon. US newspaper headline

The best cure for insomnia is to get a lot of sleep.
Senator S.I. Hayakawa of California

He is in hospital suffering from a nervous breakdown, but no doubt he will soon be better and running around like a maniac.
Simon Bates, BBC Radio 1

President Carter has painful haemorrhoids and is being treated by his physician Rear Admiral Look Ass ... Lucas.
Anon. US newsreader

Youth Hit By Train Is Rushed To Two Hospitals.
***Harrow Observer* headline**

Critics say county mental health near collapse.
***Pasadena Star News* headline**

I have been laid up with intentional flu.
Samuel Goldwyn

Women are more prone to premenstrual tension.
Dr J. McCormack

Back pain is a headache for doctors and other medical staff.
Anon. presenter, Radio Piccadilly (Manchester)

The girl has flown to America for treatment of a spinal tuna.
Anon. newsreader, BBC Radio 4

METAPHORICALLY CLICHED

Let's have some new clichés.
Samuel Goldwyn

We didn't have any metaphors in my day. We didn't beat about the bush.
Fred Trueman
(1995)

MIND GAMES

Now is the time for both players to relax, take their minds off the game, and just think about their tactics for the next set.
Ann Jones, BBC TV tennis
(1980)

This is still the greatest country in the world, if we just steel our wills and lose our minds.
President Bill Clinton

It's all just physically and mentally soul-destroying.
Geoff Boycott
(1981)

Anyone who thinks this country is turning the corner is going round the bend.
Norman Willis
(1992)

Anyone who goes to a psychiatrist needs to have his head examined.
Samuel Goldwyn

A man who was discovered by a policeman from the Royal Protection Group said he was looking for Princess Anne. He was taken to a mental hospital.
The Times

Schizophrenic Killed Herself With Two Plastic Bags.
Milton Keynes Gazette headline

MISSED ACHE

We'll do better if we capitalized on our mistakes.
Mickey Rivers

I don't make mistakes. I make prophecies which are immediately proved wrong.
Murray Walker, BBC TV motor racing

He made too many wrong mistakes.
Lawrence 'Yogi' Berra

MIXED DOUBLES

We have got to keep Henley as an international regatta and the women will have something to show some of the men.
Ron Needs, chief coach to the GB women's rowing team

And this line up for the final of the women's 400 metres hurdles includes three Russians, two East Germans, a Pole, a Swede and a Frenchman.
David Coleman, BBC TV athletics

And there's no 'I love you' message, because Steve Ovett married the girl.
David Coleman, BBC TV athletics
(1984)

The graduates of the Victorian Law Institute now are half women, half men.
Gordon Lewis
(1982)

The rolling pin throwing contest was won by Mrs Upsall ... Mr Upsall won the 100 yards dash.
Kingston Star

This unit had an estimated strength of about 2000 men, of which 300 were women.
US Intelligence Report during Vietnam War

The Bratislava girls are employing a man-to-man defence.
Anon. commentator, BBC TV basketball
(1985)

Nobody can influence me. Nobody at all. And a woman still less.
Shah of Iran

*It's difficult to play against a man ... I mean against Martina. She scares
you with her muscles.*
**Hana Mandlikova
(1984)**

MONEY MAKES THE WORD GO
ROUND

Free additional card for you and your partner to share the shame credit limit.
Co-op Bank credit card leaflet

*People in the higher income groups have greater spending power than
those with small incomes.*
**TUC statement of economics
(1956)**

*The Dante Stakes, £63,000 to the winner and Graham Greed ... Graham
Goode to read the runners and riders.*
**Brough Scott, *Racing*, Channel 4 TV
(1995)**

*If you look at the prices of transfer fees in England now, £7,000,000 for
Andy Cole is like getting him free.*
**Eric Cantona
(1995)**

It's been two ends of the same coin.
Dave Bassett

I'll fight Lloyd Honeyghan for nothing if the price is right.
Marlon Starling

*The tragedy of the Labour Party is not their aims aren't sincere. it's just
that they have this absurd obsession that high earners are rich.*
Andrew Lloyd-Webber

*Beau Jack lived to fight. Even if he didn't get paid for it, he'd still want a
fight just to release the monopoly.*
Chuck Wepner

MOTHER OF INVENTION

We're launching this innovation for the first time.
Mayor Jimmy Walker of New York

It is curious to observe the various substitutes for paper before its invention.
Isaac D'Israeli, *Curiosities of Literature*

MOTOR MOUTHS

President Banana has a 1950s Rolls-Royce Phantom, which carried Queen Elizabeth when she was here in her teens in 1947.
Zimbabwe Sunday Mail

Rolls-Royce announced today that it is recalling all Rolls-Royce cars made after 1966 because of faulty nuts behind the steering wheels.
Walter Cronkite

Ruud Gullit loping forward with that Rolls-Royce acceleration.
Pat Murphy, BBC Radio 5
(1995)

First of all Horizon on BBC 2 tonight is doing a programme about the motorcycle, 'Survival of the Fartest'.
Richard Baker, BBC TV

Traffic Will Hit Homes If Motorway Is Scrapped.
***Sutton Herald* headline**

Motorists were stuck in a five-mile traffic jam after a glue tanker overturned on the A355 at Slough, Berkshire.
Daily Telegraph

Although I braked the car went into a squid.
Daily Telegraph

Learn To Drive. Daily, Weekly & Weekend. Crash Courses Available.
Edinburgh Herald & Post

MOVING EXPERIENCE

Standing still is the same as going backwards, and when you do that people are bound to overtake you.
Ian Wolstenholme
(1978)

Mr Asquith was like a drunken man walking along a straight line, the further he went the sooner he fell.
Sir Edward Carson

Bradford, who had gone up from 200 metres to 400, found it hard going for the last 100 metres and was always going backwards.
David Coleman, BBC TV athletics

I don't think he's ever lost a race at 200 metres, except at four hundred.
David Coleman, BBC TV athletics
(1992)

If you stand still, there is only one way for you to go, and that's backwards.
Peter Shilton

We're going to move left and right at the same time.
Governor Jerry Brown of California

Please stand a little closer apart.
Michael Curtiz

Spread out in a bunch.
Noel Murphy
(1980)

They should move first base back a step to eliminate all the close plays.
John Lowenstein

MUCH ADO

Poland nil, England nil, though England are now looking better value for their nil.
Barry Davies, BBC TV football
(1989)

And now for the goals from Carrow Road, where the game ended 0-0.
Elton Welsby, ITV football

After a lifeless 0-0 draw against France :
We've not come here to entertain. We've come here to win.
Carlton Palmer
(1992)

Patrick Tambay's hopes, which were nil before, are absolutely zero now.
Murray Walker, BBC TV motor racing

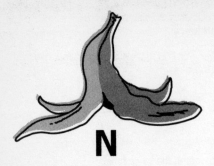

N

NAME DROPPING

But I mustn't go on singling out names ... one must not be a name-dropper, as Her Majesty remarked to me yesterday.
Norman St. John Stevas MP

Trying to introduce President Herbert Hoover :
Ladies and gentlemen. The President of the United States ... Hoobert Heever.
Harry von Zell

Trying to introduce Hubert H. Humphrey:
The great President who might have been ... Hubert Horatio Hornblower.
President Jimmy Carter
(1980)

And now over to ringside, where Harry Commentator is your carpenter.
Anon. announcer, BBC TV

Roy Race's daughter is named after Princess Diana, what is her name?
Broadcast on Greater London Radio (1994)
(This was an actual question asked of the author.)

The last player to score a hat trick in an FA Cup Final was Stan Mortensen. He even had a final named after him: 'The Matthews Final'.
Lawrie McMenemy

Your next commentator Old John Arlott from Trafford.
Rex Alston, BBC cricket

I'm getting better since I took up that Sam Carnegie course.
Bill Peterson

This is Cunis at the Vauxhall End. Cunis - a funny sort of name. Neither

one thing nor the other.
Alan Gibson, BBC cricket
(1969)

Here to speak to you on behalf of the Labour Party is Sir Stifford Crapps.
Macdonald Hobley, BBC TV
(1949)

Ieuan Evans, his name literally spells Wales.
Jonah Lomu
(1995)

People started calling me 'Fiery' because 'Fiery' rhymes with Fred, just like 'Typhoon' rhymes with Tyson.
Fred Trueman

Gary Sobers never had a nickname, he was always called Gary or the King.
Pat Pocock

I don't think there's anybody in the Browns' organization not focused on the 49ers ... I mean Chargers.
Bill Belichick (Browns' coach)

If it weren't for a name like Jethro Pugh I might be anonymous.
Jethro Pugh
(1974)

Saying goodbye to Lord Hoare :
Please give my wishes to Lady W.
Samuel Goldwyn

THE NAME REMAINS THE SAME

And now for a favourite song of mine and I'm sure yours, Everybody Loves Somebloody Sometime.
Danny Street, BBC Radio

And now Nelson Eddy sings While My Lady Sleeps with the men's chorus.
Anon. US disc jockey, Radio KALW (San Francisco)

From the fifties, a re-release for Bill Haley and the Comets, Rock Around the Cock.
Anon. US disc jockey

The next song will be I've Seen Everything When I've Seen An Elephant's Fly.
Anon. US disc jockey

I'd now like to play for you Duke Ellington's Take A Train.
Anon. US disc jockey

That was Burl Ives and his Big Cock Randy Mountain.
Anon. US disc jockey

And back from the news we come to Fever by Leggy Pee.
Don Wardell, Radio Luxembourg

And now for some music by George and Ira Gershwin. It's the Ray Noble composition But Not For Me.
Edward Cole

Yeovil Amateur Operatics Society. Book your tickets for Orphans in the Underworld by Offenbach.
Somerset and West Dorset Star
(1992)

Derek Jacobi and his brilliant performance in One Claudius.
Terry Wogan

Tonight's orchestral concert comes from the Bath Room in Pump.
Anon. presenter, BBC Third Programme
(c 1950)

At eight-fifty tonight we shall broadcast Haydn's Cremation.
Anon. presenter, BBC Radio 3

You are now going to hear The Bum of the Flightlebee.
Stuart Hibberd, BBC Radio

The young conductors tackle Beethoven's Erotica Symphony.
Kent Messenger

And that was a Symphony in J Major.
Petroc Trelawney, Classic FM Radio
(1992)

NEAR MISS

You've got to miss them to score them sometimes.
Dave Bassett

The shot from Laws was precise ... but wide.
Alan Parry, ITV football

It may have just been going wide, but nevertheless it was a great shot on target.
Terry Venables

NEW FROM OLD

A fairy dream come true.
Bill Beaumont, BBC TV rugby

Of Ian Botham's innings yesterday, soon said, least mended, I think.
Jack Bannister, BBC TV cricket

Geoff Boycott is enough of an enigma to puzzle the sphinx.
David Gower

He's been burning the midnight oil at both ends.
Sid Waddell, BBC TV darts

If you let that sort of thing go on, your bread and butter will be cut out right from under your feet.
Ernest Bevin MP

We'll jump off that bridge when we come to it.
Matt Goukas

I can smell a rat. I can see him floating in the air, but mark me. I shall nip him in the bud.
Sir Boyle Roche MP

He's coming on in fits and bounds.
Phil Liggett, Channel 4 cycling

NEW MEANING

Duke Ellington said the Battle of Waterloo was won the playing fields of Elkton.
Herman 'Babe' Ruth

It's beyond my apprehension.
Danny Ozark

I've got a great repertoire with my players.
Danny Ozark

I will perish this trophy forever.
Johnny Logan

NOT MY TYPE

John Harkes going to Sheffield, Wednesday.
New York Post
(1993)

Pakistan doomed West Indies with four wickets by the captain Wasim Akram and three by leg-spanner Mushtaq Ahmed.
The Guardian

The congregation will compromise Heads of State.
VE Day Programme
(1995)

The last batsman, Albeit Carefully, survived to lunch.
Hawkes Bay Gazette

If aunts get into your kitchen, spray the floor with paraffin.
Daily Sketch

It is considered impolite to break your beard into pieces to put in your soup.
Book of Etiquette

Some 13,500 other American citizens are now playing nursemaid to these South American rodents, envisioning wealth beyond the dreams of Ava Rice.
Pittsburgh Press

Grammer Hotline Available.
Honolulu Planet headline

Judy Oakes heaved the shop 17.84 metres to equal the UK record.
Daily Express

Prayers for Garston-based Sunday league football team urgently wanted.
Liverpool Merseymart

Mujahideen Seize Two Womens Pies.
Pakistan Times headline

Sir William McMahon was a friendly, approachable man ... [with] his almost embarrassing pubic display of devotion to his wife, Sonia, and three children.
The Times

Panorama - The Bank That Didn't Add Up. Fred Emery reports on the events leading to the biggest ever bank scandal - the collapse of BBCI.
Daily Telegraph

Tynedale Council advised that the rivers was unsuitable for bathing due to bacteria including food poisoning orgasms.
Newcastle Journal

Bedi should have been run out, but mid-on misfielded and he regained his crease after being strangled halfway down the wicket.
Daily Telegraph
(1970)

NOT AS THUNK AS YOU DRINK I AM

So you went to the hospital about your alcoholism problem. That must have taken a lot of bottle.
Judy Finnegan, *This Morning*, ITV

Irish stout, the amber nectar.
Nick Owen, *Good Morning*, BBC TV
(1995)

Stout is one of the necessaries of life.
John Daly

A liquor store was looted and police opened fire after they were stoned.
Cape Times

World's finest whisky made from Scotland's finest grapes.
Japanese whisky advert

Experts know that the alcoholic process takes longer in men, but the end reshult ies the same.
Daily Record

Alcoholic beverages are banned in Saudi Arabia. Under the country's Islamic Sharia law, those who consume alcohol are canned publicly.
Melbourne Herald

NOT THERE FAULT

Well, Ken [Norton], if you hadn't been there it wouldn't have been much of a fight.
Harry Carpenter, BBC TV boxing

Yorkshire have pulled the irons out of the fire that almost wasn't there.
Jack Bannister, BBC TV cricket
(1995)

Zola Budd, so small, so waif-like, you literally cannot see her, but there she is.
Alan Parry, ITV athletics

Slim-Fad Girl, 17, Vanishes.
The Sun headline

He just can't believe what's not happening to him.
David Coleman, BBC TV athletics

NUMBER CRUNCHING

There's only one way to go for this, 60, double ten ... or 20 double top.
Eric Bristow, TV darts

Dusty Hare kicked 19 of the 17 points.
David Coleman, Grandstand, BBC TV

If there's a 50 per cent chance we will have a repeat American League pennant win. But you've got to remember there's also a 75 per cent chance we won't.
Lawrence 'Yogi' Berra

They've got well under just over two circuits to go.
SIS horse racing commentary from Ayr
(1994)

I'm limited to the income I can have as an artist. I can only make several million a year if I'm extremely successful, but I couldn't come into the $100 million a year range ... the half billion a year range.
Jeff Koons

That'll be the 28th penalty of the game. It's the 14th against Washington and either the 13th or 14th against New York. I don't know which.
Anon. ESPN TV American football commemtator

The in-form team are Sale Moor, who have notched up six wins and nine draws in their last eight fixtures.
Sale and Altrincham Messenger

That's Hendricks 19th home run, one more and he hits double figures.
Jerry Coleman, US TV baseball

That's the fourth extra-base hit for the Padres, two doubles and a triple.
Jerry Coleman, US TV baseball

Montreal leads Atlanta by three, 5-1.
Jerry Coleman, US TV baseball

The final score after eight innings is Giants 3, Padres 2.
Jerry Coleman, US TV baseball
(Baseball has nine complete innings.)

The Padres, after winning the first game of the double-header, are ahead here in the top of the fifth, 4-0 and are hoping for a split.
Jerry Coleman, US TV baseball

At the end of six innings of play, its Montreal 5, the Expos 3.
Jerry Coleman, US TV baseball
(Montreal are the Expos.)

It's really great being 'Magic' Johnson the basketball player for eight months and then just plain Earvin Johnson for the other three.
Earvin 'Magic' Johnson

On his Wimbledon football team:
I can count on the fingers of one hand the ten games where we've caused our own downfall.
Joe Kinnear
(1993)

He's ranked number three in Britain, number four in the world. You can't get any higher.
John Lowe, TV darts

Peter Shilton conceding five goals, you don't get many of them to the dozen.
Desmond Lynam, *Grandstand*, BBC TV

On the new American football season :
I wanna gain 1500 or 2000 yards, whichever comes first.
George Rogers
(1984)

I'm sorry, but we don't have the number of the lady wearing 148.
Anon. commentator, Eurosport TV athletics
(1995)

They said it would last two rounds ... they were half wrong, it lasted four.
Harry Carpenter, BBC TV boxing

Bill Frindall has done a bit of mental arithmetic with a calculator.
John Arlott, BBC Radio cricket

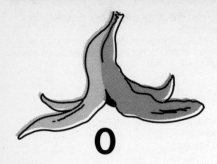

OFFICIALS SECRET ACT

I never comment on referees and I'm not going to break the habit of a lifetime for that prat.
Ron Atkinson
(1979)

I am not allowed to comment on the lousy officiating.
Jim Finks

Epsom fell foul of a bad referee who insisted on penalizing them for all their fouls
Epsom and Ewell Advertiser
(1975)

Umpire Dickie Bird is gestating wildly as usual.
Tony Lewis, BBC TV cricket

The infiltration group was composed of one third males, one third females, and one third party officials.
US Intelligence Vietnam War report

ONE MAN, ONE VETO

It's no exaggeration that the undecideds could go one way or another.
President George Bush
(1988)

Mrs Gandhi has often been accused of pandering to the Hindus to curry votes along communal lines.
The Times

Mr Ronald Brown said that the Government had been too complacent. Floating voters would expect coastal waters to at least meet the standard of the average European country.
The Times

Minnesota voters played a major role in the victory of that state's gubernatorial primary elections yesterday.
National Rifle Association press release

OLD WIVES TAILS

It has been said by some cynic, maybe it was a former president, "If you want a friend in Washington, get a dog". Well, I took them literally ... I have Barbara Bush.
President George Bush

In an article on Monday, it was stated that Stephen Reynolds is the wife of Bonnie Wheeler. Steve Wheeler is the wife of Bonnie Wheeler. We apologize for the error.
Harrisburg Daily Register

A man who almost strangled his estranged wife was given a second chance by the judge.
Gateshead Post

After trying to strangle his wife in their Ilchester home Brian John Masters called the police and asked for help.
Yeovil Western Gazette

The ladies of the Helping Hand Society enjoyed a swap social on Friday evening. Everybody brought something they didn't need. Many of the ladies were accompanied by their husbands.
Baltimore Sun

After the death, in 1982, of his wife, Gala, Salvador Dali withdrew into isolation, refusing to eat or receive visitors.
The Guardian

OFF-AIR

I've talked to you on a number of occasions about the economic problems our nation faces, and I'm prepared to tell you it's in a hell of a mess ... we're not connected to the press room yet, are we?
President Ronald Reagan

Thinking he was off air during the Olympics :
I hope the Romanian doesn't get through, because I can't pronounce her bloody name.
David Coleman, BBC TV athletics

Thinking he was off-air during a children's radio show :
I guess that'll hold the little bastards.
'Uncle' Don Carney, W.O.Radio

OPEN (AND SHUT UP)

It opens up a whole can of beans for me.
Michael York

We have really opened up a worm's nest.
Simon Bates, BBC Radio 1

OPPOSITES ATTRACT

I told you to make one longer than another, and instead you have made one shorter than the other, the opposite.
Sir Boyle Roche MP

I am accused of being impartially prejudiced.
Don King

They were standing behind each other, side by side.
Ray Warren, Channel 10 TV (Australia)
(1981)

We are examining alternative anomalies.
William Whitelaw MP
(1981)

Ball-handling and dribbling are my strongest weaknesses.
David Thompson

Strength is my biggest weakness.
Mark Snow

That's a great catch by Qasim. He's running away from the ball and just catches up with it.
Norman May, BBC Radio 3 cricket
(1982)

A remarkable catch by Yardley, especially as the ball quite literally rolled along the ground towards him.
Mike Denness

Mike Andrew's limits are limitless.
Danny Ozark

Charlie Magri has to do well against this unknown Mexican who comes from a famous family of five boxing brothers.
Harry Carpenter, BBC TV boxing

That's his style ... if you can't imitate him, don't copy him.
Lawrence 'Yogi' Berra

If we played like this every week, we wouldn't be so inconsistent.
Bryan Robson
(1990)

Marie Scott, from Fleetwood, the 17 year-old who has really plummeted to the top.
Alan Weekes, BBC TV swimming

He's like a needle in a haystack - he's everywhere!
Ray French, BBC TV rugby league

He's doing the best he can do - he's making the worst of a bad job.
Fred Trueman

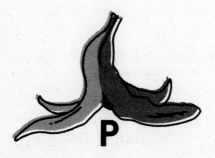

P

PEER PRESSURE

Steve Davis is acknowledged by his peers as the peerless master.
John McCririck

In eloquence of expression Adlai Stevenson had no peers and few equals.
President Richard Nixon

PER CENT AGES

You are partly 100 per cent correct.
Samuel Goldwyn

Never go for a 50-50 ball unless you're 80-20 sure of winning it.
Ian Darke, Sky TV football

Sure I've got an IQ. It's a perfect 20-20.
Duane Thomas

Ninety-five per cent of all putts which finish short of the hole don't go in.
Hubert Green

Pitching is 80 per cent of the game, the other half is hitting and fielding.
Mickey Rivers

Baseball is 90 per cent mental, the other half is physical.
Lawrence 'Yogi' Berra

You give 100 per cent in the first half of the game, and if that isn't enough, in the second half you give what's left.
Lawrence 'Yogi' Berra

The sport of wrist wrestling is about 90 per cent strength and 40 per cent technique.
Johnny Walker
(1980)

Telegram to Hollywood producer Hal Wallis :
My dear Mr Wallis. Just read Sea Wolf. You told me in your office the role would be 50-50. I am sorry to say it is just the opposite.
George Raft

PERFECTLY PERFECT

The ground at Aintree is absolutely perfect.
John Pitman, BBC TV horse racing
(1994)

We've got an absolutely perfect day here at Desert Sun stadium, and we're told it's going to be even more perfect tomorrow.
Jerry Coleman, US TV baseball

Anyway, if you ever got the perfect game of footy, it would be lousy.
Kevin Sheedy
(1981)

PERSONALLY SPEAKING

The next time I send a damn fool for something, I go myself.
Michael Curtiz

Wherever I go in this country, people know there is a problem.
Billie Snedden
(1974)

The flooding is the worst disaster in California since I was elected.
Governor Pat Brown

*The lowdown scoundrel deserves to kicked to be death by a jackass -
and I'm just the one to do it.*
Anon. Texas congressman

I'm not indecisive. Am I indecisive?
Mayor Jim Siebel of St Paul, Minnesota

*I can't tell you what I intend to to do, but I can tell you one thing, it won't
be anything rational.*
Calvin Griffith

PITCH FORK

After Brighton's goalless FA Cup draw on Barnet's notorious sloping
football pitch:
The pitch here is a great leveller.
Mike Bailey
(1982)

*If those artificial cricket pitches had stayed down they would have given
a tremendous fillip to the development of similar pitches at grass roots
level.*
Freddie Brown
(1984)

This pitch will provide plenty of up and down bounce.
Tony Greig, Channel 9 TV (Australia)
(1981)

PLANE CRAZY

On being asked how he would stop the IRA bombing campaign:
Shoot their planes down!
H. Ross Perot, US presidential candidate
(1992)

On the Gulf War:
The R.A.F. pilots described it as a turkey shoot because the Iraqis were sitting ducks.
Anon. newsreader

The pilot of the fighter, Captain Kim Yong-bae, was reported to have ejaculated shortly before the crash.
Korea Times

POLICEMAN'S LOT

During the 1968 Chicago riots:
Get this thing straight once and for all. The policeman isn't there to create disorder, the policeman is there to preserve disorder.
Mayor Richard J. Daley of Chicago

Police Found Safe Under Blanket.
Gloucester Echo headline

Referee McKercher called two policemen to the scene, and while the three were in discussion another hurtled over their heads.
Sunday Times

We are now accepted by the New Pork Police Authority who gave us training.
Dublin Evening Herald

The police are fully able to meet and compete with the criminals.
Mayor John F. Hylan of New York
(1922)

People in Preston ward are invited to a meeting at 7.15 pm tonight in St Mary's Church Hall ... to meet councillors and beat police officers.
Evening Argus

The police have infiltrated the crowd with a couple of hundred plain clothes protectives.
Ken Barrington

During live broadcast of Royal wedding:
Near to me is one of these special King's police in his Tudor finery.

These men are called beefburgers, and each one holds a halibut in his hand.
Anon. US radio announcer
(1947)

Police made six arrests, two for coin-throwing, two more for racial abuse aimed at the Gunners' black strikers Ian Wright and Kevin Campbell, a drug-pusher and a drunk.
Western Daily Press

POLITICALLY SPEAKING

UK
The Government is clutching at sport as a straw with which to beat the Russians.
Peter Lawson, ITN News
(1980)

I've just returned from 10 Drowning Street, so I know what I am talking about.
Samuel Goldwyn

CND Ducks Call For Hardline on Russia.
The Guardian headline

Butter is just the pawn in the political game of draughts.
Tony de Angeli

They would never agree to peace so long as Prussian militarism held its head above water to trample underfoot our liberties.
Sir Edward Carson, Ulster politician

*On delays in providing uniforms for the Women's Royal Naval Service :
How long is the Minister prepared to hold up the skirts of Wrens for the convenience of His Majesty's sailors?*
Dame Irene Ward MP
(1940)

Neil Kinnock is not prepared to put his button on the trigger.
Elinor Goodman

The right honourable gentleman has done what I would like you all to do - when you lay an egg, save it for a rainy day.
R. Thwaites MP
(1880)

USA
Mr Speaker, this Bill is a phony with a capital F.
Anon. US congressman

I support efforts to limit the terms of members of Congress, especially members of the House and members of the Senate.
Vice President Dan Quayle

That was consciously ambiguous in the sense that any terrorist government or terrorist movement that is contemplating such actions I think knows clearly what we are speaking of.
Alexander Haig, US Secretary of State

The only way that the Republican Party can hold the White House is to nominate a candidate who can win.
Alexander Haig, US Secretary of State

This national security strategy represents our policy for all time. Until it's changed.
Marlin Fitzwater

To hell with the public. I'm here to represent the people.
Anon. New Jersey senator

POOR LORE

The United States has so much to offer the third world war.
President Ronald Reagan
(1975)

We are not without accomplishment. We have managed to distribute poverty equally.
Nguyen Co Thach, Vietnamese foreign minister

The poor man was absolutely robbed by that accursed Tithe Bill, by fully one-tenth of his hard earnings. Nay, he was sometimes deprived of as much as one-twentieth.
Major O'Gorman MP

POT LUCK

Superstitions? I don't have any ... they're bad luck.
Jose Adeon Santos

I'm not a believer in luck, although I do believe you need it.
Alan Ball

I'm afraid it would be bad luck for me to be superstitious.
Roy Randle

Like a hole-in-one in golf, a maximum snooker break can only ever be an aimed for fluke.
John Spencer

PREDICTABLY PROMISING

I'm going to make a prediction - it could go either way.
Ron Atkinson, ITV football

I'm not going to predict what I'm gonna do, but I'm gonna come out there the winner.
Frank Bruno

Sanguillen is totally unpredictable to pitch to because he's so unpredictable.
Jerry Coleman, US TV baseball

I never predict anything and I never will do.
Paul Gascoigne

Nobody is predicting the outcome but, judging by historic precedent, it could go either way.
Robin Gould

I wouldn't be surprised at all if there's a shock result this afternoon.
John Greig

With the benefit of hindsight, are we going to get any goals in the second half?
Elton Welsby, ITV football

I promise results, not promises.
John Bond

If you can't give me your word of honour, will you give me your promise?
Samuel Goldwyn

PREGNANT PAWS

It's one of the great urban myths that people get pregnant in order to have children.
Menzies Campbell MP

Part-time mother's help required at least three afternoons per week, to help pregnant man with toddler.
Anon. Cheltenham newspaper

Condom Faults Could Lead To Dating Policy.
Bridgwater Courier, news headline

Family Planning - Please Use Rear Entrance.
Notice at Barnstaple Health Centre

No woman should be kept on the Pill for 20 years until, in fact, a sufficient number have been kept on the Pill for 20 years.
Sir Alan S. Parks
(1970)

Everyone who is for abortion was at one time a faeces.
Peter Grace

There's nothing wrong with pregnancy. Half the people wouldn't be here today if it wasn't for women being pregnant.
Sarah Kennedy

One Miami Beach matron beyond 45 is amazing and delighting her friends by having her first baby in five months.
Miami Herald

I talked to my doctor about my wife going into labour and he told me her contraceptions were an hour apart.
Mackey Sasser

Blue Peter has no plans to get rid of pregnant presenter Janet Ellis, who is due to produce an unmarried baby in August.
Nottingham Evening Post

999 men deliver baby.
Kentish Express headline

Over 400,000 women in the United Kingdom become pregnant at work every year.
Caroline Tongue
(1992)

Jimmy Connors' seeding here at Wimbledon was affected by his wife having a baby. There was some doubt about his entry.
Peter West, BBC TV tennis

There are many misconceptions about infertility.
Anon. radio discussion

PREP SKOOL

Hagi is a brilliant player, but we're not getting all psychedelic about him.
Andy Roxburgh
(1991)

On playing Cameroon in the 1990 World Cup finals:
We didn't underestimate them. They were a lot better than we thought.
Bobby Robson

Before Arsenal's game in the European Cup:
It's a tough draw. Last season Benfica played 38 games like us and lost only one, the same as us. They conceded only 18 goals, the same as us, but they scored more than we did, 89 to our 74. I don't know a lot about them.
George Graham
(1991)

PRESENT CIRCUMSTANCES

If it wasn't for golf, I'd be a caddie today.
George Archer
(1980)

If I was still at Ipswich, I wouldn't be where I am today.
Dalian Atkinson
(1992)

PULL OVERS

So often the pendulum continues to swing with the side that has just pulled themselves out of a hole.
Tony Gubba, BBC TV football

Slobodan Zivojinovic seems to be able to pull the big bullet out of the top drawer.
Mike Ingham, BBC Radio tennis

PURE GENUIS

Give me a smart idiot over a stupid genius any day.
Samuel Goldwyn

The word 'genius' isn't applicable in football. A genius is a guy like Norman Einstein.
Joe Theismann, ESPN TV

Q

Q & A

I think we're on the road to coming up with answers that I don't think any of us in total feel we have the answers to.
Kim Anderson

If you want a straight answer. It's maybe yes, maybe no.
A. C. Smith
(1989)

I wish I had an answer to that because I'm getting tired of answering that question.
Lawrence 'Yogi' Berra

There are still hundreds of question marks to be answered.
Jimmy Armfield, BBC Radio football

Poor Graham Shaw. It was there for the asking and he didn't give the answer.
Peter Jones, BBC Radio football

If you leave this question with us for three years, we will settle it tomorrow morning.
Anon 19th-century Irish MP

What's the plural of ignited?
Gaby Roslin, *Big Breakfast*, Channel 4 TV

Are there any more top swimmers in the pipeline?
Cliff Morgan, BBC Radio 5

And what shape then is the Rubik's Cube?
Peter Sissons, BBC TV

J. DANFORTH QUAYLE
(b. 1947)

If Ronald Reagan is rightly regaled as the Fred Astaire of gaffology, former Vice President Dan Quayle must be the Gene Kelly. Even in his own words, Quayle is obviously something quite extraordinary, *"People that are really very weird can get into sensitive positions and have a tremendous impact on history."* He backed this soul-searching with a self-explanatory statement, *"Verbosity leads to unclear, inarticulate things."*

Neither did he have any doubts as to his political duties, *"One word sums up the responsibility of any Vice President. And that word is ... to be prepared."* Quayle also knew exactly where he was going: *"It's a question of whether we're going forward into the future, or past to the back."*

And he had his finger firmly on the pulse of his achievements, *"We raised taxes on the American people and we put this country right into a recession."* Just in case the Republican party faithful wondered where Quayle was going, he had these words of comfort, *"We offer the party as a big tent. How we do that within the platform, the preamble to the platform, or whatnot, that remains to be seen. But that message will have to be articulated with great clarity."*

In 1992, Dan finally met his 'Waterloe' in the shape of 12-year-old New Jersey student William Figueroa. With the Vice President hosting a spelling bee in a Trenton elementary school, the schoolboy correctly spelt "potato" on the blackboard. Mr Quayle, mindful of not upsetting the student in front of the gathered news media, tried to help out in his own unique subtle way, *"That's fine phonetically, but you're missing just a little bit."* The mystified school boy was told by Quayle that potato had an "e" on the end of it. A gaffe of this magnitude was immediately broadcast around the world, but was officially played down by a White House press officer who claimed that his V-P had read the "correct" spelling off the card he had been given - written out by a school official. The whole incident was best summed up by a banner that greeted Mr Quayle on his next official visit, *"DUMPE QUAYL!"*

Despite the debacle at Trenton, Quayle refused to leave the education system well alone. *"We're going to have the best educated Americans in the world"* and *"Quite frankly, teachers are the only profession that teaches our children"* both prove Dan failed to learn his lesson.

Since spelling was not one of his best subjects, Quayle's sense of geography was also found wanting. *"Hawaii has always been a very pivotal role in the Pacific. It is in the Pacific. It is part of the United States that is an island that is right there."* Unperturbed he had another go. *"Hawaii is a unique state. It is a small state. It is a state that is by itself. It is a ... it is a different from the other forty-nine states. Well ... all states are different, but it's got a particular unique situation."*

In a short career, Dan Quayle managed to litter his language with more gaffological gems than any other who held political office, but at least he was a man of principle: *"I stand by all the misstatements."* Here are few of Dan's famous misstatements.

On John Sununu's resignation:
This isn't a man who is leaving with his head between his legs.

Republicans understand the importance of bondage between parent and child.

The loss of life would be irreplaceable.

Space is almost infinite. As a matter of fact, we think it is infinite.

Well, I ... we have said, and the platform refers to this ... that we will support a human life amendment. We do not say which human life amendment. There are a number of them. Most Americans understand the complexities of the issue of abortion. It is a very complex issue.

If we don't succeed, we run the risk of failure.

We are not ready for any unforeseen event that may or may not occur.

I will work towards the elimination of human rights in El Salvador.

Dan Quayle is not the first or the last US vice-president to suffer the slings and arrows of outrageous verbal misfortune. His successor, Democrat Al Gore was once asked to name his most inspirational U.S. President. Unfortunately, Gore's chosen role model James Knox never served as President.

Gore has also managed to show that he can mangle a well-known saying as well as his predecesor: *"We all know that leopards cannot change their stripes."*

Perhaps Quayle and Gore were too young or wet behind their ears to fully appreciate the enormity of the V-P position, as former incumbent Spiro Agnew may have suggested: *"Youth lacks, to some extent, experience."*

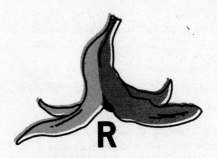

RADIO DAZE

For those of you who haven't got television sets, live commentary is on Radio 2.

David Coleman, BBC TV athletics

After winning a horse-race at Cheltenham:
Did you see me on the radio?
Tony Dobbin
(1994)

Whenever I can, I always watch the Detroit Tigers on the radio.
President Gerald Ford

What I said to them at half time would be unprintable on the radio.
Gerry Francis
(1995)

RONALD REAGAN
(b. 1911)

The one-time Hollywood actor and baseball sports announcer was once described as the great communicator for his accomplished skills in handling the media. The former US President has also been described, more accurately on evidence contained in this book, as the Fred Astaire of foot-in-mouth disease.

During his time in office, congresswoman Pat Schroeder also smelt a Reaganesque rat: *"We've got the kind of President who thinks arms control means some kind of deodorant."*

Whatever his peers thought of him, Reagan and his multitude of public-speaking gaffes provided much ammunition for humorists and journalists:

I know for a fact that Mr Reagan is not clear about the difference between the Medici and Gucci. He knows that Nancy wears one.
Gore Vidal

Washington could not tell a lie; Nixon could not tell the truth; Reagan cannot tell the difference.
Mort Sahl

What's really worrying about Reagan is that he always seems to be waiting for someone to say Cut and has no idea how they've decided the script should end.
Katherine Whitehorn
Observer
(1983)

*In the heat of a political lifetime, Reagan innocently
squirrels away tidbits of misinformation and
then, sometimes years later, casually drops
them into his public discourse, like gumballs in a quiche.*
Lucy Howard
Newsweek
(1985)

Perhaps the best comment, as far as inducting America's oldest
president into the Gaffers Hall of Fame, comes from Mark Russell:
*"Ronald Reagan is the first president to be accompanied by a Silly
Statement Repair Team."*

A shortlist of Reagan's 'silly statements' confirms the above views:

*My goal is an America where something or anything that is done to
or for anyone is done neither because of nor in spite of any
differences between them racially, religiously or ethnic origin-wise.*

*Even though there may be some misguided critics of what we're
trying to do, I think we're on the wrong path.*

*I favour the Civil Rights Act of 1964 and it must be enforced at
gunpoint if necessary.*

One of Reagan's biggest problems was in remembering names -
closely followed by remembering where he was in the world:

While in Brazil before leaving for Colombia:
*I ask you join me in a toast to President Figueiredo and the people
of Bolivia ... no, that's where I'm going.*

Welcoming President Doe of Liberia:
I'd like to extend a warm welcome to Chairman Moe.

*At the peak of his powers, Reagan managed to introduce
Princess Diana at a formal dinner as David!*

But, it wasn't just good old Ronnie who managed to get his
knickerbockers in a twist in the White Household. Second wife
Nancy has also had her memorable moments: *"I favour capital
punishment. It saves lives."*

RECYCLING PLANT

The best way to pass a cow on the road when cycling is to keep behind it.
R. J. Mecredy

The Tour de France, all those bicycles roaring through the countryside.
Andy Peebles, BBC Radio 1

The Tour de France is a totally different ballgame from English cycle-riding.
Sidney Bennett

In speed record attempts, the cyclist pedals just a few metres behind a car that break wind for the rider.
South China Morning Post

REPEAT PRESCRIPTION

Certain people are for me, certain people are pro me.
Terry Venables

Harlow Town are in their infancy compared to other giant-killing giants.
Peter Lorenzo, ITV football

Getting a wicket off the last ball was an added plus for the West Indies.
Colin Croft, BBC TV cricket
(1995)

I'm a cliff-edge guy who likes to walk on the razor's edge.
Vinnie Vechione
(1995)

Football today would certainly not be the same if it had not existed.
Elton Welsby, ITV football

If there weren't such a thing as football, we'd all be frustrated footballers.
Mick Lyons

If you [Ian St John] had stopped being the player you were, you wouldn't have been the player you've been.
Bobby Campbell

I don't know what impressive is, but Joe was impressive tonight.
Marlene Bugner, wife of boxer Joe Bugner

The Centenary Test is a unique occasion, a repeat of Melbourne 1977.
Jim Laker, BBC TV cricket
(1978)

SIR BOYLE ROCHE
(1743-1807)

The oldest gaffer in this volume served in the American War of Independence, later joined the Irish Parliament as the member for Tralee, and was created a baronet in 1782.

But the reason he is in this book is amply described in *Will's Irish Nation*. Sir Boyle Roche was *"eminently qualified by his handsome figure, graceful address, and ready wit, qualities which were set off by a frank, open and manly disposition ... but it is not generally known that it was usual for members of the cabinet to write speeches for him, which he committed to memory, and, while mastering the substance, generally contrived to travesty into language and ornament with peculiar graces of his own"*.

From the examples below, Sir Boyle was world-renowned in his own country as an inveterate perpetrator of 'bulls', as they were known in the 19th century.

Ireland is overrun by absentee landlords.

All along the untrodden paths of the future, I can see the footprints of an unseen hand.

The only thing to prevent what's past is to put a stop to it before it happens.

At present, there are such goings on that everything is at a standstill.

I concluded from the beginning that this would be the end, and I am right, for it is not half over yet.

On the relationship between England and Ireland:
I would like to see the two sisters embrace each other like one brother.

I should have answered your letter a fortnight ago, but I only received it this morning.

If I have any prejudice against the honourable Member, it is in his favour.

An alarm was given that a gang of rebels in full retreat were advancing under the French standard. They had no colours nor any drums except bagpipes.

Immediately every man in the place, including women and children, ran out to meet them.

There is not a man, woman or child present through whose mind the truth of what I have just stated has not been ringing for centuries.

Myrtle branches are so common in South Africa that they make birch brooms out of them.

He would not rest satisfied until the rocky mountains of Ireland became cultivated valleys.

Their military uniforms were all different ... chiefly green.

And finally, Sir Boyle has the answer to the question all quotes-collectors have been asking for many years: *"Who is Anon?", "... a certain anonymous author called Junius."*

There's no ball-winners, but they can all nick the ball.
Bryan Hamilton, BBC Radio 5 football
(1995)

RETURN OF THE NATIVE

Playing with wingers is more effective against European sides like Brazil than English sides like Wales.
Ron Greenwood
(1981)

Widnes, a wonderful blend of experienced stars and local youngsters like this lad Emosi Koloto.
Ray French, BBC TV rugby league
(1989)

Born in Italy, most of his fights have been in his native New York.
Desmond Lynam, BBC TV boxing

RUBBER WHERE

Condom Is Back In French Pack.
The Independent rugby headline

The present crisis was sparked off when ... the Irish Family Planning Association was fined for illegally selling condoms at the Virgin Megastore in Dublin.
Daily Telegraph

If we can just get young people to do as their fathers did, that is wear condoms.
Richard Branson

RUINS AND REMNANTS

Death on the Nile: Whodunit set on an Egyptian cruise ship on the Nile, where the real attraction is a tour of celebrated ruins, including Maggie Smith, Bette Davis and Angela Lansbury.
Anon. New York paper

In our review of Hullabaloo Over Georgie and Bonnie's Pictures, the reference to Lady Gee as 'a well bred Rembrandt' should have read 'a well bred remnant'.
Birmingham Post

S

SCORE BLIMEY!

Rally points scoring is 20 for the fastest, eighteen for the second fastest, right down to six points for the slowest fastest.
Murray Walker, BBC TV motor racing
(1981)

Two-nil is a cricket score in Italian football.
Alan Parry, ITV football
(1990)

The par here at Sunningdale is 70 and anything under that will mean a score in the 60s.
Steve Rider, BBC TV golf

We could have taken the lead before we even scored.
Peter Beardsley

SECOND HELPINGS

No one came closer to winning the world title last year than the runner-up Dennis Taylor.
David Vine, BBC TV snooker

Roscoe Tanner is one of the great runner-ups of all-time. No man could have played better.
Dan Maskell, BBC TV tennis

SELECTION

All girls playing in the Wednesday hockey match will be pinned to the notice board.
Anon. South African school

Because of the booking, I will miss the Holland game, if selected.
Paul Gascoigne

SERGEANT PEPPER'S

Widower 52, a lonely sincere genuine man who is certainly not at the pope and slippers stage of life.
Queensland Chronicle

Attractive woman, 32, new to area, looking for attractive man between 30-435 for friendship.
Nottingham Evening Post
(1995)

SET IN STONE

If Pete Rose brings the Cincinnati Reds in, they ought to bronze him and put him in cement.
Jerry Coleman, US TV baseball

I have to say that people should keep their powder dry and not get fixed in concrete on issues such as this.
Governor John Spellman of Washington

SEX

How To Satisfy A Woman Every Time is reserved for sale on a first-come first-served basis.
Carnell plc advert
(1994)

Whatever happened to the days when sex was Celia Johnson and Rachmaninov on the piano?
Imogen Stubbs

Strip Club Shock - Magistrates May Act On Indecent Shows.
Daily Mirror headline

Sexual harassment on the job is not a problem for virtuous women.
Phyllis Schlafly

At Chaddesley Court point-to-point meeting:
There is a young lady from Warwickshire waiting to take entries behind the main tent.
**Anon. tannoy announcer
(1989)**

Scorpio: A time when it shows how necessary it is for a true Scorpio male to take himself in hand. If this is done correctly there will be a real burst of activity and pleasure.
Lancashire Evening Telegraph horoscope

This is David Hamilton bidding you good night, and a reminder for you to be sure to turn off your sex.
David Hamilton

Miss Turner has set up a campaign against incestuous relationships at the house where she loves with her parents.
Enfield Gazette

Former Wimbledon champion Martina Navratilova had a surprisingly easy victory over Andrea Jaeger in the final of the Avon Tournament in Seattle. She won in straight sex.
Anon, announcer, BBC Radio

Iraqi propaganda radio broadcast during the Gulf War:
While you are away, movie stars are taking your women. Robert Redford is dating your girlfriend, Tom Selleck is kissing your lady, Bart Simpson is making love to your wife.
"Baghdad Betty"

Prasanna shot out seven batsmen for 69 runs in sixteen lovers, two of which were maidens.
Daily Telegraph

SHAPING UP

All square all the way round.
Ted Lowe, BBC TV snooker

He's faced with the eternal European triangle, which makes it very difficult to square the circle.
John Cole, BBC TV News

The Port Elizabeth ground is more of a circle than an oval. It's long and square.
**Trevor Bailey, BBC Radio cricket
(1995)**

They are getting the thin edge of the wedge by a sort of side wind.
Sir Ellis Ashmead-Bartlett

The racecourse is as level as a billiard ball.
**John Francome, *Racing*, Channel 4 TV
(1995)**

SHIPSHAPE

The boat can carry up to 150 passengers and over 14 motor vehicles. It has all the modern navigation instruments including a milk bar.
Samoa Weekly

It was the game that put the Everton ship back on the road.
Alan Green, BBC Radio football

Celtic were at one time nine points ahead, but somewhere along the road, their ship went off the rails.
Richard Park

Brian Clough wields a tight ship.
Gabriel Clark, ITV football

And the steam has gone completely out of the Spanish sails.
David Pleat, ITV football

We have permitted our naval capability to deteriorate. At the same time, we are better than we were a few years ago.
**US Secretary of Defense Caspar Weinberger
(1982)**

He's the only overseas blue rowing in both boats.
John Snagge

SIGHT AND UNSOUND

Why, that's the most unheard-of-thing I've ever heard of.
Senator Joseph McCarthy

If I wasn't talking, I wouldn't know what to say.
Chico Resch

I really didn't say everything I said.
Lawrence 'Yogi' Berra

I have a thermometer in my mouth and I am listening to it all the time.
William Whitelaw MP

Please let people know that, off the record, I'm very quotable.
Terry Donahue

Will you please lead us in a few words of silent prayer.
Bill Peterson

And Sula Bula is the winner - I heard it out the corner of my ear.
Peter O'Sullevan, BBC TV horse racing

You can hear the atmosphere.
Jonathan Agnew, BBC Radio cricket
(1995)

SIMILIES SMILIES

He is as cool as a whistle.
Tony Green, BBC TV darts
(1996)

Ian Rush is as quick as a needle.
Ron Jones, BBC Radio football

He showed everyone the right attitude and was as game as a pebble.
David Webb
(1994)

SINK OR SWIM

In this business you either sink or swim or you don't.
David Smith

It's obvious these Russian swimmers are determined to do well on American soil.
Anita Lonsborough, BBC TV swimming

I am confident that we can look forward to seeing our swimmers climbing back up the ladder to the top.
Sir Peter Heatly
(1993)

Barrie was still in the water and swimming strongly when Annal abandoned his attempt. He had still about four miles to swim as the crow flies.
Glasgow Herald

Answering Trevor MacDonald's question, "How was Mr Maxwell feeling in the last few days?":
He was in a very buoyant mood.
Richard Stott, ITN *News at Ten*

If David Wilkie goes on like this he'll be home and dry.
Alan Weekes, BBC TV swimming

A new swimming pool is rapidly taking shape since the contractors have thrown in the bulk of their workers.
Anon. East African newspaper

Once again it was the swimming pool that set the crowd alight.
**Anon. sports reporter, BBC Radio 2
(1980)**

The announcement of the disqualification was greeted by booze from spectators at the swimming pool.
Gloucester Echo

During the morning, I wandered around the lake taking photographs and while doing this fell in with Mr L. R. Singer, who was fishing. A discussion on tactics ensued.
Angler's Mail

SLOW-MOTION

Strangely, in slow-motion replay, the cricket ball seemed to hang in the air for even longer.
David Acfield, BBC TV cricket

The action replay showed it to be worse than it actually was.
Ron Atkinson, ITV football

We don't always get from slow-motion the pace at which they play.
John Barrett, BBC TV tennis

The slow-motion replay doesn't show how fast the ball was really travelling.
Richie Benaud, BBC TV cricket

The [New York] Mets has come along slow ... but fast.
Charles 'Casey' Stengel

SMASHING TIME

New Windows - Dramatic Breakthrough.
Bromley Advertiser

Rare Swansea Pottery To Go Under Hammer.
South Wales Evening Post headline

SOMETHING MORE
COMFORTABLE

It's a hot night at Madison Square Gardens, and at ringside I see several ladies in gownless evening straps.
Jimmy Powers, US radio boxing announcer

SPEECH IMPEDIMENT

There's only one thing I can say after that, and that's to clap my hands.
Trevor Bailey, BBC Radio cricket
(1981)

How can you say this and that when this and that hasn't happened yet.
Lawrence 'Yogi' Berra

I've got nothing to say. And I'll say it only once.
Floyd Smith

I couldn't let him upset me with the verbal things he was saying.
Frank Bruno
(1995)

I want to hear it so quiet we can hear a mouse dropping.
Gregory Ratoff
[When told the correct expression was 'pin', he replied, "Yes like a mouse pin dropping".]

Commentating isn't as simple as it sounds.
Ted Lowe, BBC TV snooker

The girl who lured Farrant away from his midnight rituals in Highgate Cemetery is 26 year-old Nancy O'Hoski, a sppepeech therapist from Grimsby.
Hornsey Journal

Telling it like it is means telling it like it was and how it is now that it isn't what it was to the 'is now' people.
Jill Johnston, *Village Voice*

Frozen Semen Talks.
***Action China* headline**

Hector Torrez, how can you communicate with Enzo Hernandez when he speaks Spanish and you speak Mexican?
Jerry Coleman, US TV baseball

Verbosity leads to unclear, inarticulate things.
Vice President Dan Quayle

They woulda had him at second, but he slud ... If I can't say slud into second base, what can I say? Sludded?
Jay 'Dizzy' Dean
(To cover his verbal faux pas Dean later claimed that, "Slud is something more than slid. It means sliding with great effort.")

On arriving late for a prepared speech:
Ladies and gentlemen, it is a great pleasure to be with you today. For immediate release only.
Senator Joe Montoya of New Mexico

SPEED LIMIT

The pace of the match is really accelerating, by which I mean it is getting faster all the time.
David Coleman, BBC TV football

The reason she's so fast over the hurdles is because she's so fast between them.
David Coleman, BBC TV athletics

Charlie Spedding believes in an even pace and hopes to run the second part of the race faster than the first.
David Coleman, BBC TV athletics

I don't know if I am as fast as I used to be, but I don't think I'm any slower.
Floyd Patterson

Not only has the pace been constant, it's been increasing.
Brendan Foster, BBC TV athletics
(1993)

Dr. WILLIAM SPOONER
(1844-1930)

As Dean and Warden of New College, Dr Spooner left an indelible mark on the English language ... for all the wrong reasons. Born an albino, with weak eyesight, Spooner developed a nervous tendency to transpose the beginning of separate words. The results are known as spoonerisms.

As with all great gaffers in history, Dr Spooner has also had a number of famous faux pas attributed to him. Time has blurred which are real and which were apocryphal. Below is a selection of those gaffes that have been attributed to him.

When our boys come home from France, we will have the hags flung out.

Three cheers for our queer old Dean.

For now we see through a dark, glassly..

This vast display of cattle ships and bruisers.

You will leave Oxford by the next town drain.

Son, it is kisstomary to cuss the bride.

Kinkering Congs their titles take.

Our Lord is a shoving leopard.

The defeated parliamentary candidate has just received a blushing crow.

We all know what is is to have a half-warmed fish within us.
Which of us has not felt in his heart a half-warmed fish.

Was it you or your brother who was killed in the war?

Dr. Spooner:
I want you to come to tea next week to meet Mr Casson.
Mr. Casson:
But I am Mr Casson.
Dr. Spooner:
Come all the same.

Fellow Spoonerists

Don't go away, folks, after the break we'll have a wildlife expert here, and he's going to show us a horny towel.
Johnny Carson, The Tonight Show, NBC TV

Viv Anderson has pissed a fatness test.
**John Helm, ITV football
(1991)**

Apparently the Florida vacation did him a lot of good. President Eisenhower returned today looked fanned and tit.
Walter Cronkite

In the back of Merv Hughes' mind must be that he will dance down the piss and mitch one.
**Tony Greig, Channel 9 TV (Australia)
(1981)**

Happy You Near
Frank Bough, BBC TV

I miss the thrill of riding and the sound of those hounding pooves.
Jimmy Edwards

Henry Horton's got a funny sort of stance. It looks as if he is shitting on a sooting stick.
Brian Johnston, BBC cricket

The play tells of a man haunted by a faint queer.
David Hamilton, ATV

A statement was issued last night by the British Broadcorping Castration.
**BBC Radio Home Service
(c 1950)**

There's been an effing copedemic.
Julian Wilson, BBC TV horse racing

Brian Toss won the close.
**Henry Blofeld, BBC Radio 2
(1976)**

Mr Arthur Commonly, the Bottomwealth Secretary, arrived in Lusaka...
Anon. Zambian radio newscaster

SPORTING DOUBLE ENTENDRE

Miss Stove seems to have gone off the boil.
Peter West, BBC TV tennis

There's going to be a real ding-dong when the bell goes.
David Coleman, BBC TV athletics

Bruny Surin, Canada's indoor 60 metres champion and the man helping to remove the stains left by Ben Johnson.
The Guardian

STATING THE OBVIOUS

Anything can happen in Grand Prix racing, and it usually does.
Murray Walker, BBC TV motor racing

Wembley ... which is typical Wembley.
Ron Greenwood, BBC Radio 5
(1995)

Shaquille O'Neil is so athletic because ... he's such a great athlete.
Garth Crooks, Sky TV football
(1995)

This race is all about racing.
David Coleman, BBC TV athletics

Lillian Board's great strength is her great strength.
David Coleman, BBC TV athletics

One of the great unknown champions, because very little is known about him.
David Coleman

You've got to hand it to Gonzalez, once he saw it was possible, he saw his chance and made it possible.
David Coleman

The National Museum of Photography, Film and Television is tremendously important, both in photography, film and television.
Sir Richard Attenborough

My team won't freeze in the white-hot atmosphere of Anfield.
Ron Saunders
(1980)

Football is an incredible game. Sometimes it's so incredible, it's unbelievable.
Tom Landry

Sustainable growth is growth that is sustainable
John Major, Prime Minister

Alan Shearer had a field day … all day.
Gary Lineker, *Match of the Day*, BBC TV

The Sydney Cricket Ground is as green as grass.
Colonel Pearce, Radio 2UE (Australia)

It's not so much maturity as it is growing up.
Jay Miller

He immediately got rid of the ball quickly.
Hank Stram

In motor racing the ever-present danger is always there.
John Watson, BBC TV motor racing

STIR CRAZY

Interviewing the female governor of a male prison:
Do you think the prisoners will regard you as a good screw?
Jack de Manio, BBC Radio

Has suicide become a way of life in British prisons?
Peter Glanville

As a rule, nobody instructs prisoners to do anything. If they want to do anything, they are perfectly at liberty to do it themselves
Wakefield Express

There is less doubt that Pat Jennings will appear in gaol yet again.
The Guardian

SURGICAL SPIRIT

And Kevin Keegan was there like a surgeon's knife - Bang!
Bryon Butler, BBC Radio football

There is no such thing as a surgical strike. A scalpel can turn into a club and then have a boomerang effect.
Jeremy Paxman, *Newsnight*, BBC TV

Guard dogs operating here.
Sign outside Epsom District Hospital

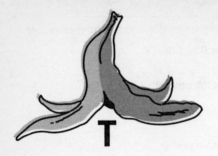

T

TAKE ONE METAPHOR

This Bill, if passed, will derail the ship of state.
Stanley Steingut

We have been hit by an avalanche of creeping paralysis.
Stanley Steingut

No one wants to say the sky is falling but I'm afraid the emperor has no clothes.
Charles Millard

We don't want to skim the cream off the crop here.
Glib Lewis

TALL STORIES

I don't think there is anyone bigger or smaller than Maradona.
Kevin Keegan

All right, line up alphabetically according to your height.
Charles 'Casey' Stengel

He is even smaller in real life than he is on the track.
David Coleman, BBC TV athletics

Larry Moffet is 6-3 and 190 pounds. Last year he was 6-6.
Jerry Coleman, US TV baseball

T A X

We raised taxes on the American people and we put this country right into a recession.
**Vice President Dan Quayle
(1992)**

Sin tax? What will those fellers in Washington think of next?
Jay 'Dizzy' Dean

T E A M   W O R K

The Baltimore Orioles team is experiencing many problems this year collectively as a group.
Ken Brett, US TV baseball

Wally Joyner just completed an unassisted double play by himself.
Ken Brett, US TV baseball

T H A T ' S   E N T E R T A I N   M E A N T

The one-man show you do, is that just you?
Terry Wogan

In response to complaints from the touring company of Oh Calcutta, the nude revue - that they were suffering from the cold, the theatre management has agreed to install fan-heaters.
**Anon. newsreader, BBC Radio 4
(1981)**

The Mermaid Theatre's pantomime is Treasure Island, and in the title role Frank Windsor.
Steve Allen

Club operators know a box-office hit when they see one, and that's why Jim Davidson appears in Luton for only one night tomorrow.
Luton Evening Post

T I M E   G E N T L E M E N ,   P L E A S E

Tony Gwynn was named player of the year for April.
Ralph Kiner

If a week is a long time in politics, it's an equinox in football.
**Stuart Hall
(1987)**

It's a battle with himself and with the ticking finger of the clock.
David Coleman, BBC TV athletics

David Bedford is the athlete of all time in the 1970s.
David Coleman, BBC TV athletics

Her time was four minutes and 13 seconds, which she is capable of.
David Coleman, BBC TV athletics

Alan Pascoe could have won the gold but he simply ran out of time.
David Coleman, BBC TV athletics

The late start is due to the time.
David Coleman

Thank you for evoking those memories, particularly of days gone by.
Mike Ingham, BBC Radio

It's permanent for the time being.
Roberto Kelly

There comes a time in every man's life, and I've had plenty of them.
Charles 'Casey' Stengel

We have been boyhood friends all of our lives.
Mayor Richard J. Daley of Chicago

The game will start at 5pm Pacific Coast League Daylight time.
Ralph Kiner, US TV baseball

Watch the time, it gives you a good indication of how fast they are running.
Ron Pickering, BBC TV athletics

She's dragged the javelin back into the 20th century.
Ron Pickering, BBC TV athletics

The three-day marathon rafting event takes place on May 28, 29, 30, 31 on the one hundred mile stretch of water from Hay-on-Wye to Chepstow.
Macclesfield Express Advertiser

All the fashion buyers in Arnotts Department Store are looking forward to Irish Week, which runs from 16-28 October.
Irish Times

Players prefer the FA Cup because it's the end of season curtain raiser.
Peter Withe, GMTV
(1994)

The annual balance sheet is now being prepared annually instead of quarterly as it used to be before the Second World War.
Heckmondwike Herald

Give me two years and I'll make her an overnight star.
Harry Cohn

The way he's swinging the bat, he won't get a hit until the 20th century.
Jerry Coleman, US TV baseball

TOOLS OF THE TRADE

West Ham Debate What They Can Do To Change Dicks.
***The Times* headline**

During the England v West Indies Test match:
The bowler's Holding, the batsman's Willey.
Brian Johnston, BBC cricket
(1976)

The Tories have been under some pressure to toughen up their party political broadcasts. Mr Heath, Mr Macleod and Mr Peter Walker accordingly reached for their choppers.
The Guardian

Mellor Wants Chopper Movement Monitored.
The Borough News
(1995)

You either have regulations or you do not. If the British Railways Board attempt to do something to my member, I will move right in to back him up.
Sid Weighell, *Sunday Telegraph*

TREAD BARE

You were treading where no man fears to go.
Ron Pickering

The hurdles we had to climb were traditionally untrodden ... so we were blazing new trails all the time.
Anon. power expert

TRUTH FAIRY

There are two kinds of truth: real truths and made-up truths.
Mayor Marion Barry of Washington DC

I don't want to tell you any half-truths unless they're completely accurate.
Dennis Rappaport

Sometimes I am stranger than the truth.
John Riggins

Half the lies our opponents tell about us are not true.
Sir Boyle Roche MP

I was not lying. I said things that later on seemed to be untrue.
President Richard Nixon

Thus, the black lie, issuing from the base of his throat, becomes a boomerang to his hand, and he is hoist by his own petard, and finds himself a marked man
Wisconsin newspaper editorial

U

UNFORGETTABLE

On the England and New Zealand teams being introduced to the Queen at Lords:
It's obviously a great occasion for all the players. It's a moment they will always forget.
Ray Hudson
(1969)

Harry Bath is having a very memorable and forgettable year.
Ray Warren, Channel 10 TV (Australia)
(1981)

130

UNSEEN

You could see he was going to play a disguised lob there.
Dan Maskell, BBC TV tennis

Mike Rafter again doing the unseen which the crowd so much relish.
Bill MacLaren, BBC TV rugby

The crowd think that Todd handled the ball ... they must have seen something that nobody else did.
Barry Davies, BBC TV football
(1975)

Some reporters said I don't have any vision. Well, I don't see that.
President George Bush

UNTOWARD CHRISTIAN SOLDIERS

I didn't know Onward Christian Soldiers was Christian song.
A. M. Pate

They're known by their Christian names in Turkey.
John Motson, BBC TV football
(1987)

Ah yes, Mohammed, that's one of the most common Christian names in the world.
David 'Kid' Jensen

The Arabs and Jews should settle their differences like good Christians.
Warren Austin, US ambassador to the UN
(1948)

UPS and DOWNS

On his success in TV's 'Superstars':
I still think I could be the best pole vaulter in Britain, but I'm in danger of falling between two stools.
Brian Hooper
(1982)

I went up the greasy pole of politics step by step.
Michael Heseltine MP

It's another notch in the rung on the slippery slope towards anarchy.
George Gavin

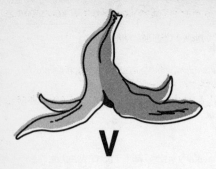

V

VALUE FOR MONEY

He came on a free transfer and has been giving good value for money.
Clive Allen

We're overpaying him, but he's worth it.
Samuel Goldwyn

A nickel ain't worth a dime any more.
Lawrence 'Yogi' Berra

VEGETABLE

I can see the carrot at the end of the tunnel.
Stuart Pearce
(1992)

This is the real carrot at the end of the rainbow.
Paul Lyneham, ABC TV (Australia)

There was still the big prize money hanging there like a carrot waiting to be picked.
David Vine

Venison and Butcher, they're both as brave as two peas in a pod.
John Sillett

United trooped off with their pride in taters.
Sunday People

He went down like a sack of potatoes and made a meal of it.
Trevor Brooking, BBC TV football

Approximately 80 per cent of our air pollution stems from hydrocarbons released by vegetation.
President Ronald Reagan
(1980)

On being told a boxer was a strict vegetarian:
I don't care what religion he is. If he doesn't get moving, he's gonna lose this fight.
Gil Clancy, US TV boxing

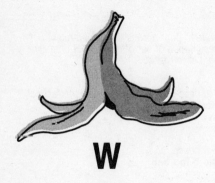

W

WALK DON'T RUN

Walkout By 150 Cripples.
Yorkshire Post headline

Limb Centre Hit By a Walkout.
Cumberland News headline

WALK TALL

The Massachusetts Minutemen are not tall in terms of their height.
Dan Bonner, CBS TV basketball

WAR AND PEACE

This new atom bomb is dynamite.
Samuel Goldwyn

*There is good news on the war front tonight. From North Africa comes
word that Allied troops have stopped the advances of Hitler's Pansy
Division.*
**Anon. newsreader, BBC Radio
(1942)**

During the Vietnam War:
*I've lived under situations where every decent man declared war first and
I've lived under situations where you don't declare war. We've been
flexible enough to kill people without declaring war.*
Lt. Gen. Lewis B. Hershey

The IRA are deadly serious about a cessation of violence.
John Hume MP

During the Korean War:
*Should the Red hordes continue to pour across the Yalu, it might not
only render impossible the resumption of our offensive, but conceivably
could eventuate in a movement in retrograde.*
Gen. Douglas MacArthur

*The Take That tour appears to have been planned with all the tactical
skills of Rommel and his Desert Rats.*
**Paula Yates, *Daily Express*
(1994)**

Paul McGrath, the old Irish war-house.
**John Champion, BBC Radio 5 football
(1995)**

*Under the overall supervision of the Hirohito's uncle, Prince Asaka,
Hirohito's bonsai-shouting imperial army embarked on six weeks of
wholesale atrocities and barbarism.*
New York Times

WATER WORKS

On Queen Victoria opening the Forth Bridge:
The Queen herself graciously pissed over the magnificent edifice.
The Times

*Ah, the Queen has now left the bridge and gone down below for some
reason or other ... and now I can see water coming through the side of
the ship.*
**John Snagge, BBC Radio
(1939)**

MURRAY WALKER

In recent years, BBC TV sports viewers, deprived of their regular dose of David Coleman in live matches or meetings, have turned to another equally proficient foot-in-mouth specialist. Murray Walker is now the BBC TV's GP maestro (GP = Gaffe Perpetrator). Motor sport in the UK would not be the same without Murray over- cranking the vocal gears, as Clive James has also noticed.

"Even in moments of tranquillity, Murray Walker sounds like a man whose trousers are on fire."
Clive James
Glued To The Box

Whether time will dub Murray's offerings as Walkerisms we shall have to wait and see. As part of his claim to the gaffe hall of fame, the following will have to be taken into consideration, and possibly used against him.

The lead car is absolutely unique, except for the one behind it, which is identical.

An Achilles heel for the McLaren team this year, and it's literally the heel because it's the gear box.

He's watching us from hospital with his injured knee.

Whatever is wrong with Arnoux's engine would be irremediable in the time it takes to do it.

Michael Schumacher, virtually pedalling his Benetton back with his fists.

And now the boot is on the other Schumacher.

You can cut the atmosphere with a cricket stump.

You can't see the digital clock because there isn't one.

We now have exactly the same situation as at the beginning of the race, only exactly opposite.

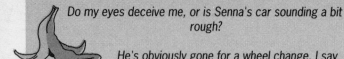

Do my eyes deceive me, or is Senna's car sounding a bit rough?

He's obviously gone for a wheel change. I say obviously because I can't see it.

Just under ten seconds for Nigel Mansell. Call it nine point five seconds in round figures.

If your water contains sediment, let it stand, then strain through a clean muslim.
Hereford Times

I was unhappy, but it's over, done ... water under the dam.
Cal Ripken Sr.

Steve Davis with his sip of water, part of his make-up.
Ted Lowe, BBC TV snooker

WEAR IT WELL

Trousers are now allowed to be worn by ladies on the course. But they must be removed before entering the clubhouse.
Sign at Irish golf club

Lindwall has now finished his over, goes over to the umpire, takes his sweater and strides off.
Rex Alston, BBC Radio cricket

The rule was that a girl would not be allowed in the bra without a man.
Exeter Express and Echo

On retiring from boxing and taking up motor racing:
I'm well protected. I've got inflammable boots, inflammable gloves and an inflammable suit.
Barry McGuigan

National League umpires wear inside check protectors.
Jerry Coleman, US TV baseball

Janet Reger talks about the ups and downs of the ladies underwear business.
Anon. presenter, Woman's Hour, BBC Radio 4

A new film by Jacques Cousteau, the famous French underwear explorer.
Channel 13 TV (New York)

Arnold Palmer, usually a great putter, seems to be having trouble with his long putts. However he has no trouble dropping his shorts.
Anon. US golf commentator

The Spirella corset factory is closing because the bottom has dropped out of the market.
Anglia TV

The bridesmaid wore a dress in the same material as the bridge.
Shropshire Journal.

The bride was given away by her father who wore a white ballerina length dress of rose patterned lace.
Cambrian News

I recently bought a pair of arousers in a boutique.
Dublin Evening Press

WEATHER FORK ASKED

Blizzards, snow drifts and icy roads have wrecked the County Council Highways budget and plunged Surrey into chaos. Taken by surprise by one of the most severe winters of the century, finance chiefs are gritting their teeth.
Surrey Advertiser

You can't beat the tidal wave when the avalanche comes down the mountain.
**Robert Kilroy-Silk, BBC TV
(1993)**

India is the finest climate under the sun but a lot of young fellows come out here, and they drink and they eat, and they drink and they die; and then they write home to their parents a pack of lies, and say it's the climate that killed them.
Sir Colin Campbell

This year we have had the hottest summer of the year and the coldest winter of the year.
**Derek Thompson, *The Morning Line*, Channel 4
(1995)**

The wind at Candlestick Park is blowing with great propensity.
Ron Fairly, US baseball announcer

I'm glad to say that this is the first Saturday in four weeks that sport will be weather-free.
David Coleman, *Grandstand*, BBC TV

The weather will be colder. There are two reasons for this. One is that the temperature will be lower.
BBC Radio
(1969)

A tipsy-turvy sort of night over Scotland.
Bill Giles
(1995)

An end is in sight for the severe weather shortage.
Ian Macaskill, BBC TV weather
(1995)

At Ascot today the heat is quite hot.
Judith Chalmers, BBC TV horse racing
(1978)

It's another wonderful day here at Sabina Park, the wind shining and the sun blowing gently across the field.
Ray Lawrence
(1960)

After a letter had dropped off the weather chart:
Well, that was the forecast and we're sorry for the F in Fog.
Julian Pettifer

There is some possibility of showers tonight ... although it is probable there will be no rain.
Los Angeles Express

The game in St Louis has been halted in the fourth inning because of rain. I'll bet they have the jacuzzis going there.
Jerry Coleman, US TV baseball

Folks, this is perfect weather for today's game. Not a breath of air.
Curt Gowdy, US TV baseball

It's a perfect day here in Australia, glorious blue sunshine.
Christopher Martin-Jenkins, BBC Radio 3 cricket
(1979)

I selected a shady nook and basked in the sunshine.
R. J. Mecredy

In terms of the Richter Scale, this defeat was a Force eight gale.
John Lyall

The news from Guadalajara, where the temperature is 96 degrees, is that Falcao is warming up.
Brian Moore, ITV World Cup football

I can't see, unless the weather changes, the conditions changing dramatically.
Peter Alliss, BBC TV golf
(1995)

Man, it was tough. The wind was blowing about 100 degrees.
Mickey Rivers

The winds of change are tasting good at the moment.
Anne Diamond

Fog and smog rolled over Los Angeles today, closing two airports and slowing snails down to a traffic pace.
Manchester Evening News

Turner pulls into second with a sun-blown double.
Jerry Coleman, US TV baseball

WEIGHTS AND MEASURES

The new Haitian baseball cannot weigh more than four ounces or less than five.
Jerry Coleman, US TV baseball

The European Cup is 17 pounds of silver and is worth its weight in gold.
Brian Moore, ITV football

That's inches away from being millimetre perfect.
Ted Lowe, BBC TV snooker

On Jonathan Edward's world record triple jump:
It is exactly sixty feet ... and one quarter of an inch.
Stuart Storey, BBC TV athletics
(1995)

The cup of our trouble is running over, but, alas, is not yet full.
Sir Boyle Roche MP

WHIRLED RECORDS

That's the fastest time ever run, but it's not as fast as the world record.
David Coleman, BBC TV athletics

Ingrid Kristiansen has smashed the world record. Truly amazing. Incidentally, this is a personal best for Ingrid.
David Coleman, BBC TV athletics

There he is the fastest man in the world this year. Other men may have run faster, but he did it when it mattered.
David Coleman, BBC TV athletics
(1992)

WHO DAT?

Hi folks! I'm Gerry Gross
Jerry Coleman, US TV baseball
(Gerry Gross is another San Diego baseball announcer.)

Well hi folks, and welcome to New York Yankee baseball and I'm Bill White.
Phil Rizzuto, US TV baseball

And there's the unmistakable figure of Joe Mercer ... or is it Lester Piggott.
Anon. commentator, ITV horse racing
(1981)

The Cup touches so many people. It's a fair bet that, by the end of today, players you never heard of will be household names, like that fellow who scored for Sutton against Coventry last season.
Bobby Campbell, Chelsea match programme
(1990)

WINNING ISN'T EVERYTHING

There'll only be one winner now, in every sense of the word.
David Coleman, BBC TV athletics

He won the bronze medal in the 1976 Olympics, so he is used to being out in front.
David Coleman, BBC TV athletics

Panetta was the silver medallist in the European championships when he led all the way.
David Coleman, BBC TV athletics

Nottingham Forest are having a bad run, they've lost six matches without winning.
David Coleman, BBC TV football

The Olympic spirit is to go out and beat the other athletes of the world, not to live with them.
John Stockton
(1992)

Wekesa has never won a match at Wimbledon ... in fact he's never played here
Anon. commentator, Channel One TV tennis
(1995)

When we lose I can't sleep at night. When we win I still can't sleep at night, but when you win, you wake up feeling better.
Joe Torre

I'm not afraid of Jack Nicklaus. If you play better than him, you can beat him.
Tom Weiskopf

The judges have given a draw, but we'll be back in a couple of minutes to talk to the loser.
Reg Gutteridge, ITV boxing

A winning formula is not something you can write an equation for.
Maggie Brown

The Seattle Supersonics are 19-0 in games they've led after the fourth quarter.
Rich Moxley, US TV basketball

The reason the New York Mets have played so well at Shea Stadium this season is that they have the best home record in baseball.
Ralph Kiner, US TV baseball

Sutton has lost 13 games in a row without winning a ball game.
Ralph Kiner, US TV baseball

The Pittsburgh Pirates won eight of their 102 losses against the New York Mets last year.
Ralph Kiner, US TV baseball

Anytime the Detroit Pistons scores more than 100 points and holds the other team below 100 points, they almost always win.
Doug Collins, US TV basketball

I was in a no-win situation, so I'm glad I won rather than lost.
Frank Bruno

It's not one of Bruno's fastest wins, but it's one of them.
Harry Carpenter, BBC TV boxing

Don't you guys think for a minute that I'm going to take this loss standing down.
Bill Peterson

If in winning the game we only finish with a draw we would be fine.
Jack Charlton

If you're going to lose, you might as well lose good and proper and try to sneak a win.
Ted Dexter

Winning doesn't really matter as long as you win.
Vinny Jones

Football's not just about scoring goals. It's about winning.
Alan Shearer
(1995)

If we're gonna win, we have to play up to and beyond our potential. We're capable of doing that.
Don Nelson

Winning isn't the end of the world.
David Pleat, ITV football

Should Taylor fail to win this one his already slim chances will look anorexic.
The Guardian

Rosenborg have won 66 games, and they've scored in all of them.
Brian Moore, ITV football
(1995)

WORD COUNT

Men I want you just thinking of one word all season. One word and one word only, Super Bowl.
Bill Peterson

Madison Square Garden is one very big word.
Franklin Jacobs
(1978)

One word sums up probably the responsibility of any vice president. And that word is ... to be prepared.
Vice President Dan Quayle

America has a word that says it all: You never know!
Joquain Andujar

There's only one word for that ... magic darts.
Tony Green

If there is one word to describe Atlantic City, it's Big Business.
Donald Trump
(1989)

In two words - im possible.
Samuel Goldwyn

Boys, I only have two words to say to you. Just two words. Believe in yourself.
Bernie Burke

Jan Stejskal only knows three words of English: my ball, away and one other.
Ray Wilkins
(1991)

Juninho will only need to learn three words of English: Pound, Thank You and Bye Bye.
Jan Aage Fjortoft
(1995)

There's an unmentionable four-letter word in Northern Ireland's World Cup vocabulary... defeat.
Daily Mirror

WORD POWER

I'm exuberated ... I think that's the word.
Phil Frasch

Progression is not proclamation nor palaver. It is not pretence nor play on prejudice. It is not of personal pronouns, nor perennial pronouncement. It is not perturbation of a people passion-wrought, nor a promise proposed.
President Warren G. Harding

We offer the party as a big tent. How we do that within the platform, the preamble to the platform, or whatnot, that remains to be seen. But that message will have to be articulated with great clarity.
Vice President Dan Quayle

My life is a living testimony and is an incongruity and a contradiction to what America has hitherto asked for success.
Don King

WORLD IN ACTION

I was asked to come to Chicago because Chicago is one of our 52 states.
Raquel Welch

The woman was arrested on request of Chicago authorities and is held in Communicado in a hotel.
Louisville Times

Wes Parker was originally born in Chicago.
Curt Gowdy, US TV baseball

We must restore to Chicago all the good things it never had.
Mayor Richard J. Daley

The streets are safe in Philadelphia, it's only the people who make them unsafe.
Mayor Frank Rizzo

On being asked to name the capital of New York:
New Jersey?
Tori Spelling

The national lottery is morally repugnant to millions of people, not only in the United States, but also in the 24th Congressional District.
Congressman Alfred Santangelo of New York

Detroit or Motor Town as they call it for short.
Linda Lewis, BBC Radio 4
(1994)

Hawaii has always been a very pivotal role in the Pacific. It is in the Pacific. It is part of the United States that is an island that is right there.
Vice President Dan Quayle
(1989)

Hawaii is a unique state. It is a small state. It is a state that is by itself. It is a ... it is a different from the other 49 states. Well ... all states are different, but it's got a particular unique situation.
Vice President Dan Quayle
(1992)

Ferguson is a Fijian, a native of Fiji ... he's from Tonga, actually.
Chris Rea, ITV World Cup rugby
(1995)

At a banquet given by Anwar Sadat:
To the great people and government of Israel - excuse me, of Egypt.
President Gerald Ford
(1975)

An Arab country, like Ireland, is a place where the remarkable seldom happens and the impossible is of frequent occurrence.
Daily Telegraph

And in the Cup-Winners Cup, Spurs will play either Eintracht or Frankfurt.
Alistair Burnett, ITN News at Ten
(1982)

A reception was held at Langford's Hotel, Hove and the couple are honeymooning in grease.
Shoreham Herald

Two Fast Germans escaped to West Berlin during the night in the second escape of the week.
Hong Kong Standard

On promoting a fight in Venezuela:
Great, that's the Italian city with the guys in the boats, right?
Murad Muhammad
(1992)

China is a big country, inhabited by many Chinese.
President Charles de Gaulle

The Republic of China, back in the Olympic Games for the first time.
David Coleman, BBC TV Olympics

And with an alphabetical irony Nigeria follows New Zealand.
David Coleman, BBC TV athletics

The French are not normally a Nordic skiing nation.
Ron Pickering, BBC TV skiing

Life is not worth living unless you have a choice of all the gloriously unhygienic things which mankind, especially the French portion of it, has lovingly created.
Prince Charles

On the difficulties of adjusting to playing football and living in Italy:
It was like being in a foreign country.
Ian Rush

In Willie DeWit, we have an all-American boy, even though he is a Canadian.
Billy Joe Fox

Ottawa is not a foreign game.
Patrick McGilligan

I mostly stayed around the house. But I did take a hunting trip to one of those Canadian proverbs.
Jim Gantner

Ballarat is the fairest city south of the hemisphere.
Edward Murphy

Sade is currently in Spain, but we've put in a trans-Atlantic call and here she is.
Mike Smith, BBC Radio 1

With EuroDisney soon to be built just across the Channel, British theme parks will just seem Mickey Mouse affairs.
Neil Walker

WOULD FOR THE TREES

In a private bar there is a box of mahogany panels that are believed to have come from a sycamore tree that stood on the site.
Southend Standard-Recorder

We should be barking up the wrong tree to go down that road.
Professor Patrick Myndfoot

Sometimes big trees grow out of acorns. I think I heard that from a squirrel.
Jerry Coleman, US TV baseball

THE WRITER WRIT

I'm astounded by people who take 18 years to write something. That's how long it took that guy to write Madame Bovary, and was that ever on the bestseller list?
Sylvester Stallone

On being asked if he was going to write his autobiography:
On what?
Chris Eubank
(1995)

When I see these guys write all this macho stuff I want to smash their heads.
John Turturro

On a Hollywood baseball biopic:
This is a good story. Usually they just take your biology and rewrite.
Harry Coyle

We do not have censorship. What we have is a limitation on what newspapers can report.
Louis Nel, South Africa's Deputy Minister of Information

I'm going to cancel my prescription to that publication.
Bob Stanley

While I write this letter, I have a pistol in one hand and a sword in the other.
Sir Boyle Roche

This book has too much plot and not enough story.
Samuel Goldwyn

Shakespeare has not only shown human nature as it is, but as it would be found in situations to which it cannot be expressed.
Samuel Johnson

I've only heard what I read in the papers.
Frank Burns

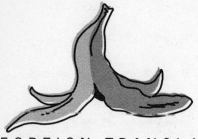

FOREIGN TRANSLATIONS

Sign in Indian bookshop:
Spoken English sold here.

East Asian textbook:
Correctly English in 100 Days.

Majorca shop:
Here Speeching American
English Well Talking

Hotels
From a rulebook for Japanese hotel chambermaids:
Light pranks add zest to your services, but don't pull the customers' ears.

Sun'n'Sand Hotel car park, Bombay:
Cars should be parked in take-off position.

Atlas Hotel, Cairo:
Take the elevator and press the 12th bottom.

Bucharest hotel:
The lift is being fixed for the next day. During that time we regret you will be unbearable.

Belgrade hotel lift:
To move the cabin, push button of wishing floor. If the cabin should enter more persons, each-one should press number of wishing floor. Driving is then alphabetically by natural order. Button pressing retaining pressed position shows received command for visiting station.

Tokyo hotel:
Is forbidden to steal hotel towels. If you are not a person to do such a thing is please not to read notis.

Leipzig hotel:
Do not enter the lift backwards, and only when lit.

Irish hotel:
Please do not lock the door as we have lost the key.

Japanese hotel:
Cooles and Heates: If you want just condition of warm in your room, please control yourself.

Hotel Caravel, Sorrento:
We would ask you to contact the concierge immediately if you should have any problem regarding the hotel and its services, so that we are able to do all possible to give you complete satisfaction, and make stay a happy one. Please don't wait last minutes, then it will be too late to arrange any inconveniences.

Japanese hotel:
Sports jackets may be worn but no trousers.

Swiss hotel:
If you have any desires during the night pray ring for the chambermaid.

Viennese hotel:
In case of fire, do your utmost to alarm the hotel porter.

Japanese hotel:
You are invited to take advantage of the maid.

Austrian skiing hotel:
Not to preambulate the corridors in the hours of repose in the boots of ascencion.

Swiss hotel:
Because of the impropriety of entertaining guests of the opposite sex in the bedroom, it is suggested that the lobby be used for this purpose.

Swiss hotel:
Do you wish to change in Zürich? Do so at the hotel bank.

Moscow hotel:
If this is your first visit to Moscow, you are welcome to it.

Norwegian hotel:
Ladies are requested not to have children in the bar.

Parisian hotel:
Please leave your values at the front desk.

Victory Hotel, Guangdong, China:
Please deposit your valuables in the management.

Athens hotel:
Visitors are expected to complain at the office between the hours of 9 and 11am daily.

Yugoslav hotel:
The flattening of underwear with pleasure is the job of the chambermaid.

Istanbul hotel:
To call room service, please open door and call "Room Service".

French hotel:
If you hear the alarm, quickly leave the room, shut the door and go downstairs without losing your temper.

Sun Hotel, Zimbabwe:
To speak to another guest in another room. Please follow these instructions:
First floor - add 250 to the room number and dial.
Second, Third and Fourth floors - dial the number required.
Fifth floor - subtract 250 from the room number and dial, except Room 542 whose number is 294.

Clothes
Rome laundry:
Ladies, leave your clothes here and spend the afternoon having a good time.

Japanese shop:
Our nylons cost more than common, but you'll find they are best in the long run.

Bangkok dry cleaners:
Drop your trousers here for best results.

Paris clothes shop:
Dresses for street walking.

Majorca launderette:
Drop your trousers here for the best results.

Swedish shop:
Fur coats made for ladies from their own skin.

Hong Kong clothes shop:
Ladies may have a fit upstairs.

Rhodes tailor shop:
Order your summers suit. Because is big rush we will execute customers in strict rotation.

Travel
Thai travel office:
Would you like to ride on your own ass?

Bombay taxi sign:
Licensed to curry four passengers.

Czech travel office:
Take one of our horse-driven tours. We guarantee no miscarriages.

Danish flight operator:
We take your bags and send them in all directions.

Japanese car rental firm:
When passenger of foot heave in sight, tootle the horn. Trumpet him melodiously at first, but if he still obstacles your passage then tootle him with vigour.

Japanese road guide:
Beware of greasy corner where lurk skid demon. Cease step on, approach slowly, round cautiously, resume step on gradually.

If wandering horse by roadside obstacle your path, beware that he do not take fright as you pass him. Gom soothingly by, or stop by the roadside till he pass away.

At the rise of the hand of the policeman, stop rapidly. Do not pass him or otherwise disrespect him.

Thai taxi:
Safety First! Please putting on your seat belt and preparing for accident.

Katmandu travel station:
The comfort of our buses is next to nun.

Spanish Airlines sick bag:
Bag to be used in case of sickness or to gather remains.

Indonesian tour guide:
If we are lucky we will see duck doys bringing their ducks to town, men massaging their cocks in the road ... Don't miss it on your visit to Bali.

Medical
Hong Kong dentist:
Teeth extracted by the latest methodists.

Romanian surgery:
Specialist in women and other diseases.

Food and Drink
Chinese restaurant:
For sanitation purposes, please sanit in the pots provided and not on the floor.

Chinese restaurant:
Serve you with hostility.

Chinese restaurant:
Dreaded veal cutlet.

Chinese restaurant:
Cold shredded children and sea blubber in spicy sauce.

Tokyo bar:
Cocktails for ladies with nuts.

Tokyo restaurant:
For those of our customers who are vegetables, we are able to offer a plate of hot mixed vegetables.

Tokyo restaurant:
Butered saucepans and fried hormones.

Hong Kong restaurant:
Sweat from the trolley

Hong Kong food label:
We are specializing in making dried-pork and pork-sliced. The staff is under expert supervision and hygienically packed.

Vietnamese restaurant:
Pork with fresh garbage.

Djakarta hotel:
Smoked Solomon.

Malaysian restaurant:
Seafood brought in by customers will not be entertained.

Bali restaurant:
Toes with butter and jam.

French café:
Persons are requested not to occupy seats in this cafe without consummation.

Swiss restaurant:
Our wines leave you nothing to hope for.

Hungarian restaurant:
Utmost of chicken.

Swiss café:
Special today: no ice-cream.

Spanish restaurant:
Kidneys of the chef.

Italian hotel:
Visitors are requested not to throw coffee or other matter into basin. Why else it stuffs the place inconvenient for the other world.

Belgian café:
Cream Dognuts.

Four-star Cairo Hotel:
Cock in Wine Sauce
French Fried Ships.

Japanese bakery :
Dogs and croissant petty brunch.

Hong Kong restaurant:
Stink and Kidney Pie.

Polish restaurant:
Salad of firm's own make.
Limpid red beet soup with cheesy dumplings in the form of a finger.
Roasted duck let loose.
Beef rashers beaten up in the country peoples fashion.

Polish tourist leaflet:
As for the tripe served at the Metropol Hotel, you will sing its praises to your grandchildren on your deathbed.

Israeli resaturant:
Turdy Delight.

Cairo hotel:
Please try the tarts of the house available for your delight on the trolley.

Istanbul airport:
Terminal soup.

Tunis hotel:
Brick with Egg and Tunafish.

Yemeni hotel:
Fish Rotty and Spaghetti Bolognese.

Chinese restaurant in Sydney:
Stuffed eggplant with minced crap

Cape Cod hotel:
We offer in-room tea services and donuts in season.

Mexican hotel:
The manager has personally passed all the drinking water served here.

Other mistranslations
Hong Kong shop:
For your convenience, we recommend courteous, efficient self-service.

Italian campsite:
By order of the Police, one obliges the frequenters of the camping to wearing bath-costumes that are not giving offence to the Morals.

Finnish washroom:
To stop the drip, turn cock to right.

Emporio Disco, Mexico:
Members and Non-Members Only.

Black Forest campsite:
It is strictly forbidden on our Black Forest camping site that people of a different sex, for instance men and women, live together in one tent unless they are married with each other for that purpose.

Chinese mistranslation of "Pepsi Comes Alive" slogan:
Pepsi brings your ancestors back from the grave.

Japanese ski lodge:
Foreigners are requested not to pull cock in bath.

Bangkok temple:
It is forbidden to enter a woman even a foreigner if dressed as a man.

Budapest Zoo:
Please do not feed the animals. If you have any suitable food, give it to the guard on duty.

Moscow cemetery:
You are welcome to visit the cemetery where famous Russian and Soviet composers, artists, and writers are buried daily, except Thursday.

Soviet Weekly :
There will be a Moscow exhibition of arts by 15,000 Soviet Republic painters and sculptors. These were executed over the last two years.

Italian Guide book:
Describing a musuem: Attention must be drawn to a collection of beetles, modestly encased in drawers, but one wonders at the exhibition.

Maltese Guide book:
Although every possible care has been taken, I do not accept responsibility for inoccurancies.

Annapurna, Nepal signpost:
Before you defecate make sure there is no latrine around.

WHAT DID THEY MEAN?

The answers appear on page 155.

1. Introducing Rev. Jesse Jackson :
This country needs a spear-chucker, and I think we've got him up on this podium.
Eugene Dorff

2. *Gerald Ford was a Communist.*
President Ronald Reagan

3. *Jimmy Carter speaks loudly and carries a fly-spotter.*
**President Gerald Ford
(1976)**

4. *What a waste is it to lose one's mind, or not to have a mind is very wasteful. How very true.*
Vice President Dan Quayle

5. *If you give a man a fish he will fish for a day.*
**Vice President Dan Quayle
(1992)**

6. *For seven and a half years, I've worked alongside President Reagan. We've had triumphs. Made some mistakes. We've had some sex.*
President George Bush

7. *Some of the greatest Oedipuses in the world have been built by Donald Trump.*
Don King

8. We need laws that protect everyone. Men and women, straights and gays, regardless of sexual perversion.
Bella Abzug

9. Drinking is the cure for psoriasis.
US Secretary of Health Donna Shalala
(1993)

10. I am providing you with a copulation of answers to several questions raised.
Mayor Marion Barry of Washington DC

11. I don't want to get into that but Mike Tyson has got a whole new set of banisters.
Don King

12. We will always have wealthy people who have a condom in the South of France.
Caroline Miller

13. On behalf of you all, I want to express my appreciation for this tremendously warm recession.
Ron Brown
(1992)

14. Ted Williams is a big clog in the Red Sox machine.
Lawrence 'Yogi' Berra

15. We shall reach greater and greater platitudes of achievement.
Mayor Richard J. Daley of Chigago

What they meant:

1. *He claimed he meant straight shooter.*
2. *He meant congressman.*
3. *He meant fly swatter.*
4. *He probably meant to say "A mind is a terrible thing to waste" but, then, who knows!*
5. *He meant eat for a day.*
6. *He meant setbacks. Bush later said:"I feel like the javelin thrower who won the toss and elected to recieve.*
7. *He probably meant edifices.*
8. *She meant persuasion.*
9. *She meant cirrhosis.*
10. *He meant compilation.*
11. *He meant barristers.*
12. *She meant condominium.*
13. *He meant reception.*
14. *He meant cog.*
15. *He possibly meant plateaux, or latitudes, or altitudes.*

Entries in bold refer to
special box features

A

ABC-TV 41
Abzug, Bella 155
Acfield, David 119
Action China 121
Adamson, Tony 22
Agnew, Jonathan 118
Agnew, Spiro 107
Allen, Clive 132
Allen, Dominic 10
Allen, Steve 127
Alliss, Peter 64, 139
Alston, Rex 77, 84, 136
Anderson, Kim 104
Anderson, Sparky 64
Andrew, Rob 26
Andujar, Joquain 142
de Angeli, Tony 99
Angler's Mail 119
Anglia TV 137
Arblaster, David 13
Archer, George 103
Arlott, John 91
Armfield, Jimmy 104
Arnold, Andrea 9
Ashdown, Paddy 7
Ashmead-Bartlett, Sir Ellis
117
Atkinson, Dalian 103
Atkinson, Ron 23, 61, 92,
101
Attenborough, Ron 124
Austin, Warren 131

B

Bacall, Lauren 6
"Baghdad Betty" 116
Bailey, Mike 17, 97
Bailey, Trevor 34, 116, 120
Baker, Richard 82
Ball, Alan 100
Baltimore Sun 93
Bamford, Maurice 41
Bangladesh Times 11
Banham, John 42
Bannister, Jack 87, 90
Barlow, Gary 35
Barnes, Dale 64
Barnes, Wally 39
Barrett, John 119
Barrington, Ken 5, 98
Barry, Marion 129, 155
Barrymore, Michael 20
Bassett, Dave 15, 81, 87
Bates, Simon 14, 23, 78, 94
*Bath & West Evening
Chronicle* 8
Beardsley, Peter 114
Beaumont, Bill 87
Beck, Barry 11

Beer, Lionel 41
Belfast Telegraph 21
Belichick, Bill 85
Belinksy, Bo 17
Belton, Mr 40
Benaud, Richie 119
Bennett, Sidney 110
Bennett, Winston 65
Berra, Dale 26
Berra, Lawrence "Yogi" 17,
        26, 28, 40, 44, 45,
        47, 53, 60, 80, 90,
        95, 96, 104, 117,
        120, 132, 155
Best, George 16
Bevin, Ernest 18, 87
Birmingham Post 113
Blackmore Vale Magazine 45
Blofeld, Henry 123
Boise Idaho Statesman 68
Bond, John 101
Bonner, Dan 133
Border, Allan 16
Borough News 129
Bottomley, Virginia 20, 32
Bough, Frank 23, 44, 123
Boulton, Adam 14
Bowman, John 29
Boxer, Barbara 32
Boycott, Geoff 79
Branson, Richard 113
Brazil, Alan 13
Brett, Ken 6, 127
Bridgwater Courier 102
Bristol Evening Post 44, 49,
        52
Bristow, Eric 90
Britton, Tony 62
Bromley Advertiser 120
Brooken, Rod 46
Brooking, Trevor 16, 62,
        132
Brooks, Claire 36
Brown, Freddie 97
Brown, Jerry 83
Brown, Jock 64
Brown, John 13
Brown, Maggie 141
Brown, Pat 97
Brown, Ron 155
Bruno, Frank 6, 9, 13, 20,
        101, 120, 141
Buckingham Star 40
Bugner, Marlene 110
Burke, Bernie 143
Burnett, Alistair 145
Burns, Frank 147
Bush, George 7, 19, 21, 23,
        32, 37, 47, 75, 92,
        93, 131, 154
Butler, Bryon 39, 125

C

Calcutta Express 48
Calcutta Telegraph 32
Campbell, Bobby 110, 140
Campbell, Sir Colin 137
Campbell, Menzies 101
Campbell, Nicky 74
Cambrian News 137
Canaan New Advertiser 28
Cantona, Eric 81
Cape Times 89
Carney, "Uncle" Don 93
Carpenter, Harry 12, 21, 23,
        39, 90, 91, 95,
        141
Carr, Ian 8
Carson, Sir Edward 82, 99
Carson, Johnny 123
Carter, Jimmy 41, 84
Cartland, Barbara 68
Chalmers, Judith 138
Champion, John 134
Charles, Prince 145
Charlton, Jack 142
Charters, Robin 45
Cheltenham Echo 45
China Daily 21
Clancy, Gil 133
Clark, Gabriel 117
Clinton, Bill 79
Coe, Sebastian 40
Coetzee, Gerrie 37
Cohen, Erma 41
Cohn, Harry 68, 129
Cole, Edward 28, 86
Cole, John 116
Coleman, David 6, 22, **24-
        25**, 26, 34, 37, 42,
        50, 53, 57, 58, 62,
        73, 80, 83, 90, 93,
        107, 121, 124,
        126, 128, 138,
        139, 140, 145
Coleman, Jerry 14, 15, 17,
        27, 39, 53, 58, 64,
        91, 96, 101, 115,
        121, 126, 129,
        136, 138, 139,
        140, 146
Collins, Doug 141
Collins, Joan 60
Connally, John 29
Connor, Eugene 37
Conteh, John 34
Cooper, Terry 10
Corbett, James J. 12
Cormack, Sir Magnus 59
Corry, Martin 14
Cox, Mark 6
Coyle, Harry 146
Cozier, Tony 57
Crawford, Frank 52
Croft, Colin 110
Cronkite, Walter 82, 123
Crooks, Garth 124

Croxford, Alan 62
Crum, Danny 51
Cumberland News 133
Currie, Edwina 17
Curtiz, Michael 15, **29**, 83, 97
Curzon, Lord 70

D

Daily Californian 28
Daily Express 12, 45, 88
Daily Mirror 12, 115, 143
Daily Post 50
Daily Record 89
Daily Sketch 88
Daily Telegraph 9, 11, 16, 38, 53, 65, 68, 82, 89, 113, 116, 145
Daley, Richard J. 28, 98, 128, 144, 155
Dalton's Weekly 49
Daly, John 89
Daniels, A. 14
Darke, Ian 22, 96
Daugherty, Duffy 17, 35
Davies, Barry 83, 131
Daytona Daily News 5
Dean, Jay "Dizzy" 23, 40, 121, 127
Deedes, William 44, 47
Dempsey, Paul 13
Denness, Mike 94
Dent, John 42
Derby Evening Telegraph 48
Dexter, Ted 142
Diamond, Anne 139
Diaz-Ballart, Lincoln 68
Dickinson, Sandra 46
Dillon, James M. 61
Dinkins, David 75
D'Israeli, Isaac 82
Dobbin, Tony 108
Dolan, Terry 44
Dole, Elizabeth 72
Dole, Robert 21
Donahue, Terry 118
Dorff, Eugene 154
Dublin Evening Herald 98
Dublin Evening Press 137
Duff, Mickey 40
Duffield, David, 9
Duncan, Dave 43
Dundee, Angelo 76
Dunn, John 7

E

East Anglian Daily Times 53
Eastern Evening News 75
Eden, Sir Anthony 19
Edinburgh Advertiser 18, 48
Edinburgh Herald & Post 82
Edinburgh Evening News 48
Edmonds, Ray 10

Edwards, Jimmy 123
Egyptian Gazette 20
El Paso Times 5
Enfield Gazette 116
Engineer, Farokh 12
Epsom & Ewell Advertiser 92
Estefan, Gloria 33
Evans, Maureen 35
Evening Argus 98
Evening Gazette 49
Evening News 15
Evening Standard 30
Evening Star 48
Essex Country Standard 9
Eubank, Chris 44, 146
Ewbank, Weeb 16
Exeter Express & Echo 136
Express & Echo 60

F

Fairly, Ron 6, 137
Faulkner, Stuart 16
F.A. Year Book 60
Feaver, William 45
Feller, Bob 38
Ferguson, Ronald 38
Ferragamo, Vince 23
Ferrie, Tom 65
FIFA News 31
Finks, Jim 92
Finnegan, Judy 89
Fitzwalter, Marlin 100
Fjortoft, Jan Aage 143
Fleming, Ian 64
Ford, Gerald 33, 52, 58, 108, 144, 154
Forfar Courier 42
Foster, Brendan 121
Fox, Billy Joe 145
Fox, Samantha 46
Francis, Gerry 11, 60, 108
Francome, John 6, 117
Frasch, Phil 143
French, Ray 22, 65, 95, 112
Frisch, Frank 31
Fresno Bee 28

G

Gantner, Jim 145
Garagiola, Joe 26
Gascoigne, Paul 101, 115
Gateshead Post 93
de Gaulle, Charles 145
Gavin, George 131
Gibson, Alan 85
Gidley, Andrew 65
Giles, Bill 138
Gladstone, William E. 14, 32
Glanville, Brian 125
Glasgow Evening Times 48
Glasgow Herald 118
Glendenning, Raymond 62
Glick, Larry 43,

Gloucester Echo 98, 119
Goldwyn, Samuel 7, 11, 17, 23, 26, 44, **54-55**, 78, 79, 85, 96, 99, 101, 103, 132, 134, 143, 147
Goodman, Elinor 99
Gore, Al 107
Goukas, Matt 87
Gould, Bobby 101
Goward, Pru 18
Gowdy, Curt 138, 144
Gower, David 87
Grace, Peter 102
Grade, Lew 68
Grade, Michael 9
Graham George 103
Graham, Herol 13
Gratian, Harry 22
Graveney, David 70
Gray, Mike 6
Greaves, Jimmy 16, 76
Green, Hubert 96
Green, Alan 117
Green, Tony 52, 118, 142
Greenhof, Brian 50
Greenwood, Ron 75, 112, 124
Greig, John 15, 75, 101
Greig, Tony 31, 97, 123
Griffith, Calvin 97
Groom, Simon 10
The Guardian 9, 10, 15, 19, 36, 57, 64, 65, 69, 88, 93, 99, 124, 129, 142
Gubba, Tony 103
Gulf Daily News 18
Guerrero, Pedro 10, 26
Gutteridge, Reg 141

H

Haig, Alexander 47, 100
Hall, Stuart 127
Hamilton, Bryan 62, 112
Hamilton, David 116, 123
Hampstead & Highgate Express 49
Handyman 11
Harding, Warren G. 143
Harris, Labron 34
Harris, Rolf 60
Harrisburg Daily Register 93
Harrison, Benjamin 51
Harrod, Dominic 22
Harrogate Advertiser 9
Harrow Observer 78
Hastings Observer 45
Hatch, Orrin 19
Hatcher, Wilson 43
Hawkes Bay Gazette 88
Hayakawa, S.I. 78
Heatly, Sir Peter 118

Hebert, F.E. 20
Heckmondwike Herald 128
Helm, John 10, 65, 123
Hendrick, Mike 67
Hendricks, Elrod 58
Hereford Times 136
Hershey, Lewis B. 134
Heseltine, Michael 131
Hibberd, Stuart 86
Hickel, Walter 23
Higgins, Alex 58
Hill, Jimmy 42, 75
Hirschfield, Abe 60
Hobley, Macdonald 85
Holden, Andy 42
Hong Kong Standard 145
Honolulu Planet 88
Hooper, Brian 131
Hornsey Journal 120
Howard, Michael 70
Hudson, Ray 130
Hume, John 134
Humphrey, Hubert H. 4, 58
Hurd, Douglas 30
Hutton, Sir Len 16
Hylan, John F. 98

I

Ilford Recorder 34
The Independent 113
Indian Express 13
India Weekly 74
Ingham, Mike 103, 128
Inkster, Julie 73
Irish Press 35, 49
Irish Times 128
Irish Ulster Magazine 63
Isle of Wight County Press 35

J

Jackson, Alan 22
Jacobs, Franklin 142
Jameson, Derek 33, 77
Jensen, David 131
Jersey Evening Post 31
Jessel, Toby 42
Johns, Hugh 40
Johnson, Earvin "Magic" 91
Johnson, Samuel 74, 147
Johnston, Brian **71-72**, 123, 129
Johnston, Jill 121
Johnstone, Derek 13
Jones, Ann 79
Jones, Emlyn 22
Jones, Peter 10, 47, 63, 104
Jones, Ron 63, 118
Jones, Vinnie 142

K

Kaufman, Philip 50
KDKA-TV 37
Keegan, Kevin 76, 126
Kelly, Richard 36
Kelly, Roberto 128
Kennedy, Sarah 102
Kent Courier 29
Kent Messenger 60, 86
Kentish Express 102
Kentish Times 11
Kerr, Graham 9
Kilroy(-Silk), Robert 137
Kiner, Ralph 73, 127, 128, 141
King, Don 52, 94, 143, 155
King, Larry 35
Kingston Informer 48
Kingston Star 80
Kinnear, Joe 91
Kinnock, Neil 70
Kissinger, Henry 51
Knapp, Jimmy 36
Koch, Ed 19
Koons, Jeff 90
Korea Times 98
Kraft, Jack 53

L

Laidlaw, Renton 22
Laker, Jim 110
LaMotta, Jake 73
Lancashire Evening Telegraph 116
Landry, Tom 124
LaRussa, Tony 26
Law, Denis 76
Lawrence, Lennie 47
Lawrence, Ray 138
Lawson, Peter 99
Le Bon, Simon 20
Lee, Gordon 53
Leicester Mercury 46
Leigh Journal 34
Lemass, Sean 17
Levy, Peter 59
Lewis, Gib 75, 126
Lewis, Gordon 80
Lewis, Linda 144
Lewis, Tony 92
Licht, Frank 43
Liggett, Phil 87
Lineker, Gary 125
Linley, Jimmy 61
Liverpool Merseymart 88
Lloyd, David 37
Lloyd, Greg 46
Lloyd-Webber, Andrew 81
Logan, Johnny 34, 44, 88
Lomu, Jonah 85
Long Island Press 49
Lonsborough, Anita 118
Lord, Malcolm 14
Lorenzo, Peter 62, 110

Los Angeles Express 138
Loughran, Angus 61
Louisville Times 144
Lowe, John 91
Lowe, Ted 14, 15, 21, 39, 116, 120, 136, 139
Lowenstein, John 83
Luton Evening Post 127
Lyall, John 138
Lynam, Desmond 34, 57, 91, 112
Lyneham, Paul 132
Lyons, Mick 110

M

MacArthur, Douglas 134
McCarthy, Joseph 117
Macaskill, Ian 138
McClaren, Bill 40
McCormack, Dr. J. 78
McCririck, John 95
MacDonald, J. Ramsay 14
MacDonald, W.L. 20
MacEntee, Sean 11
McGauley, James 5
McGee, Frank 41
McGilligan, Patrick 17, 145
McGuigan 136
Maclaren, Bill 65, 131
McMenemy, Lawrie 84
McNail, Ian 63
MacPherson, Archie 47
MacVeigh, Jeremiah 61
Macclesfield Express Advertiser 128
Madden, John 16
Maddox, Lester 47
Maitland, Lady Olga 6
Major, John 53, 125
Manchester Evening News 139
Mandlikova, Hana 81
de Manio, Jack 125
Manley, Albert 5
Mara, Wellington 4
Marfin, G.L. 62
Marks, Dr 44
Marler, Robin 64
Martin-Jenkins, Christopher 77, 138
Maskell, Dan 21, 26, 114, 131
Mason, Gary 76
May, Norman 94
Mayo, Simon 63
Mecredy, R.J. 110, 138
Meechan, Evan 37
Meier, Dieter 12
Melbourne Herald 89
Memphis Commercial Appeal 10
Mercer, David 37
Miami Herald 102

INDEX

Michael, George 14
Michelmore, Guy 57
Millard, Charles 126
de Mille, Cecil B. 68
Miller, Caroline 155
Miller, Jay 125
Miller, Keith 51
Milner, Sir Frederick 30
Milton Keynes Gazette 79
Minneapolis Star Tribune 78
Minter, Alan 65
Montoya, Joe 121
Moon, Rupert 13
Moorcroft, David 12
Moore, Brian 13, 23, 28,
    59, 76, 77, 139,
    142
Moore, John T 7
Morgan, Cliff 33, 104
Morley, Julia 12
Morning Post 43
Morning Star 35
Mosey, Don 44
Motson, John 14, 22, 52,
    131
Moxley, Rich 141
Muhammad, Murad 145
Mulcahy, Richard 44
Murphy, Alex 12
Murphy, Edward 146
Murphy, Noel 83
Murphy, Pat 82
Murray, Jenni 20
Myndfoot, Patrick 146

N

National Rifle Association 93
Navratilova, Martina 12
Neal, Phil 44, 70
Nebraska Smoke-Eater 33
Needs, Ron 80
Nel, Louis 146
Nelson, Don 142
Nevitt, Chuck 73
Newcastle Journal 89
*Newhall Signal & Saugus
Enterprise* 63
News of the World 20
New York Post 88
New York Times 134
Nixon, Donald 70
Nixon, Richard 5, 52, 95,
    130
Norman, Greg 73
North Wales Advertiser 48
North Wales Quids-In 49
Nottingham Evening Post
    102, 115

O

O'Brien, William Smith 42
O'Gorman, Major 100
O'Neill, Ann 17, 31

O'Sullevan, Peter 65, 118
Oaksey, Lord John 76
Oman, Akhbar 73
Owen, Nick 44, 89
Oxford Mail 77
Ozark, Danny 88, 94

P

Paisley, Ian 28
Pakistan Times 88
Palmer, Carlton 83
Park, Richard 117
Parkin, David 32
Parks, Sir Alan S. 102
Parry, Alan 17, 87, 90, 114
Parsons, Nicholas 33
Pasadena Star News 78
Pasternak, Joe 35
Pate, A.M. 131
Patterson, Floyd 121
Paxman, Jeremy 125
Pearce, Colonel 125
Pearce, Stuart 132
Pearson, Stuart 50
Peebles, Andy 110
Perkins, John 70
Perkins, Ray 16
Person, Chuck 15
Perot, H. Ross 98
Peters, Jon 68
Petersfield Post 49
Peterson, Bill 18, 84, 141,
    142
Pettifer, Julian 138
Philadelphia Bulletin 35
Pickering, Ron 12, 128,
    129, 145
Pickles, James 52
Pinkus, Steve 61
Pitman, John 61, 96
Pittsburgh Press 88
Pleat, David 117, 142
Pocock, Pat 64, 85
Pollard, Eve 58-59
Portsmouth Evening Echo 12
Powers, Jimmy 120
Price, Vincent 17
Procaccino, Mario 37
Pugh, Jethro 85

Q

Quayle, J. Danforth 4, 46,
    47, 50, 60, 100,
    105-107, 121,
    127, 142, 143,
    144, 154
Queensland Chronicle 115
Quisenberry, Dan 51

R

Raft, George 96

Randle, Roy 100
Rapf, Harry 15
Rappaport, Dennis 129
Ratoff, Gregory 35, 120
Rea, Chris 144
Reagan, Nancy 19, 109
Reagan,Ronald
    10,59,93,100,
    108-109,
    133, 154
Redhead, Brian 11, 19
Resch, Chico 117
Rhodesia Herald 28
Ribblesdale, Lord 75
Richmond Times 52
Ricketts, Tony 72
Rider, Steve 114
Riggins, John 130
Ripken Sr., Cal 136
Rivers, Mickey 64, 80, 96,
    139
Rizzuto, Phil 47, 74
Rizzo, Frank 144
Robertson, Max 59
Robson, Bobby 31, 39, 103
Robson, Bryan 63, 95
Roche, Sir Boyle 7, 11, 15,
    20, 72, 87, 94,
    111-112, 130,
    139, 147
Rogers, George 91
Rose, Pete 64
Roslin, Gaby 104
Rowell, Jack 5
Roxburgh, Andy 60, 102
Royle, Joe 38
Rush, Ian 145
Rusher, William 70
Russell, Lord Charles 31
Ruth, Herman "Babe" 87
Rutigliano, Sam 70
Ryder, Steve 17

S

St. John Stevas, Norman 84
Salcombe Gazette 48
*Sale & Altrincham
Messenger* 90
Samoa Weekly 117
Sanders, David 40
Satangelo, Alfred 144
Santos, Jose Adeon 100
Sasser, Mackey 102
Saunders, Ron 124
Schacht, Hjalmar 53
Schlafly, Phyllis 116
Scotland Sunday Standard
    45
Scott, Brough 81
Sevenoaks News 15
Sexton, James 43
Shah of Iran 80
Shalala, Donna 155
Sharp, Rhod 45

159

Shatner, William 32
Shearer, Alan 142
Sheedy, Kevin 96
Sheene, Barry 46
Sheldon, Jo 65
Shields, Brooke 33
Shilton, Peter 83
Shoreham Herald 145
Shropshire Journal 137
Shropshire Star 35, 53
Siebel, Jim 97
Sillett, John 132
Singapore Times 6, 43
Singer, Isaac Bashevis 47
Sioux Falls Argus Leader 43
Sissons, Peter 104
Skinner, Richard 47
Smith, A.C. 104
Smith, David 118
Smith, Floyd 120
Smith, Harvey 62
Smith, Mike 146
Smith, Steve 5
Snagge, John 76, 117, 134
Snedden, Billie 97
Sneva, Tom 33
Snipes, Renaldo 13
Snow, Mark 94
Solihull Times 62
Somerset & West Dorset
        Star 86
South China Morning Post
        110
Southend Evening Echo 29
Southend Standard-Recorder
        146
South London Press 30
South Wales Evening Post
        120
Spelling, Tori 144
Spellman, John 115
Spencer, John 101
Spinks, Leon 46
Spooner, William 57, **122**
Sporting Life 16
Stallone, Sylvester 146
Stanley, Bob 147
Stanley, Edward 32
Starling, Marlon 81
Starmer-Smith, Nigel 23
Steingut, Stanley 126
Stengel, Charles "Casey" 14,
        119, 126, 128
Stewart, Ed 33
Stirling News 49
Stockton, John 141
Stokes, Sir John 59
Storey, Stuart 139
Stott, Richard 119
Stram, Hank 125
Straw, Jack 34
Street, Danny 85

Stubbs, Imogen 115
The Sun 90
Sunday Chronicle 52
Sunday People 53, 132
Sunday Times 98
Surrey Advertiser 137
Sutton Herald 82

T
Tarkanian, Jerry 57
Thach, Nguyen Co 100
Thatcher, Carol 69
Theismann, Joe 103
Thomas, Duane 96
Thomas, Sir Jeremy 13
Thompson, David 94
Thompson, Derek 137
Thompson, Tommy 7
Thwaites, R. 99
The Times 9, 15, 18, 37,
        49, 53, 77, 78, 79,
        89, 92, 129, 134
Tokyo Times 33
Tongue, Caroline 102
Toronto Globe 32
Torre, Joe 141
Trelawney, Petroc 86
Trevino, Lee 32
Trueman, Fred 79, 85, 95
Trump, Donald 143
Tuigamala, Va'iga 67
Turner, Ken 38
Turturro, John 146
Tutu, Desmond 15

V
Vechione, Vinnie 110
V.E. Day Programme 88
Venables, Terry 6, 14, 23,
        41, 59, 87, 110
Vine, David 26, 114, 132
Voice of America 7
von Zell, Harry 84

W
Waddell, Sid 87
Waddell, William 45
Waddle, Chris 16
Wade, Virginia 17, 46, 61
Wakefield Express 125
Walker, Jimmy 81
Walker, Johnny 53, 96
Walker, Murray 69, 80, 83,
        114, 124, **135-
        136**
Walker, Neil 146
Wall, Christy 36
Wallace, George 12

Wall Street Journal 51
Wandsworth Times 48
Ward, Dame Irene 99
Wardell, Don 86
Warren, Ray 94, 130
Warrenton Democrat 28
Watford Evening Echo 48
Watkins, Alan 18
Watson, John 125
Webb, David 118
Weekes, Alan 95, 119
Weighell, Sid 129
Weinberger, Caspar 117
Weiskopf, Tom 141
Welch, Raquel 144
Welsby, Elton 63, 83, 101,
        110
Wepner, Chuck 81
West, Peter 102, 124
Western Daily Press 99
Western Evening Herald 41
Western Mail 32
Western Morning News 14
West Wales Guardian 41
Whitbread, Fatima 42
Whitelaw, William 11, 59,
        94, 118
Whiteside, Norman 76
Wilcox, Toyah 22
Wilder, Douglas 7
Wilkins, Ray 143
Wilkinson, Howard 16
Willis, Norman 79
Wilson, Julian 123
Withe, Peter 128
Wogan, Terry 86, 127
Wolstenholme, Ian 82
Wolverhampton Express &
        Star 49
Wood, Leon, 74
Woodward, Sandy 70
Worcester Source 49
World in Runcorn 32
Worthing Trader 48

Y
Yates, Paula 134
Yeovil Western Gazette 93
York, Michael 94
Yorkshire (Evening) Post 41,
        59, 62, 133
Youngblood, Jack 63

Z
Zimbabwe Sunday Mail 82